In Praise of Steam

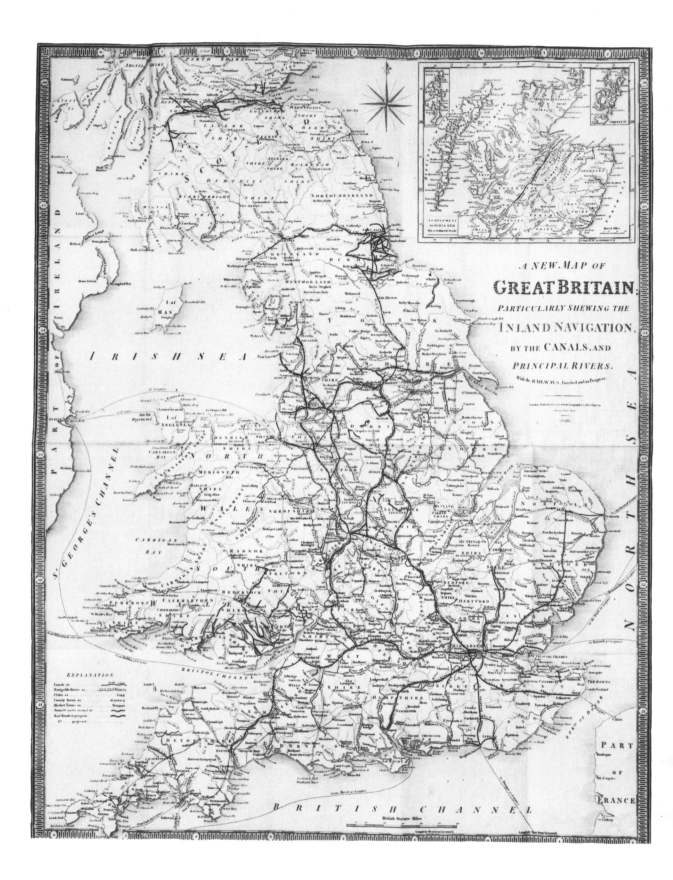

A NEW MAP OF

GREAT BRITAIN,

PARTICULARLY SHEWING THE

INLAND NAVIGATION,

BY THE CANALS, AND

PRINCIPAL RIVERS.

With the RAILWAYS, Finished and in Progress.

London, Published by JOHN TEGG Geographer to His Majesty.
1840.

EXPLANATION

In Praise of Steam

Robert Adley

Have I not in my time heard lions roar?
Have I not heard the sea, puff'd up with winds,
Rage like an angry bear chafed with sweat?
Have I not heard great ordnance in the field,
And heaven's artillery thunder in the skies?

The Taming of the Shrew
Act I Scene II

BLANDFORD PRESS
POOLE · DORSET

Books by the same author:
BRITISH STEAM IN CAMERACOLOUR 1962–68
IN SEARCH OF STEAM
THE CALL OF STEAM
TO CHINA FOR STEAM (*English and Chinese*)
ALL CHANGE HONG KONG

First published in the UK 1985 by Blandford Press,
Link House, West Street, Poole, Dorset, BH15 1LL

Copyright © 1985 Robert Adley

Distributed in the United States by
Sterling Publishing Co., Inc.,
2 Park Avenue, New York, N.Y. 10016

British Library Cataloguing in Publication Data

Adley, Robert
    In praise of steam.
    1. Locomotives—Great Britain—History
    I. Title
    625.2′61′0941   TJ603.4.G7

ISBN 0 7137 1626 6

Typeset by Keyspools Ltd., Golborne, Lancs.
Printed in Great Britain
by Purnell & Sons Ltd., Paulton, Nr. Bristol, Avon.

Dedication

Yet again to the tolerance of Jane,
and to the memory of Derek Cross

Contents

Introduction

If familiarity really breeds contempt, then these words will remain unread, this book remaindered. As I set out to write the introduction to my fifth railway book – as yet untitled – it is with humility but satisfaction. Whilst my photographs of working steam herein are proffered for the first time, neither the format of this book, nor indeed the style of my literary effort, can truly be described as original. Yet therein lies the rub: it is nostalgia, remembrance and familiarity, rather than novelty, originality or surprise that steam railway enthusiasts crave. For this I am extremely grateful.

If my task in this introduction was to be the avoidance of repetition then my earlier books would be spread out in front of me. Yet my rapport with the broad army of railway enthusiasts guides my pencil steadfastly along the track. Clearly my supply of unpublished photographs is not unlimited, but hopefully the confidence of publisher and author will not disappoint you, the customer. When sketching out the chapter titles for this book, my choice was inevitably partly influenced by the availability of material. I know I repeat myself in apologising for the fact that my self-description is 'railway enthusiast with camera', rather than 'railway photographer'. Indeed I relish the occasional lofty criticism of my photography from the 'professionals' just as much as I value the letters of praise and thanks that seem to land on my desk with splendid regularity from less pretentious but equally well-qualified readers.

Did I say 'task'? If, in my arrogance I may claim some familiarity between my pen and lens, and your eyes and interest, it is my certain knowledge, born of book-sales, print-runs and indeed Public Lending Right returns, that tells me what I mean, and what you expect me to mean, when I write *In Praise of Steam*. That spirit still survives on British Rail, personified by men like James Lake. Before introducing James Lake, however, I am obliged, yet again, to try to answer the unanswerable conundrum

— 'What is the appeal of Steam?' Indeed what is the appeal of the railway itself?

Who will write a book entitled *In Praise of Roads*? Or *In Praise of Cars*? Railways create, roads destroy. Who wants to photograph a car 'on shed' — at a garage . . . Who cares where any car, or bus, *was*, on a given date? Who knows or cares when a car was scrapped? Where it was scrapped? At which 'dump' it finished up? Merely to ask such questions is to answer them, and to differentiate totally between the quintessential, eternal appeal of a 'Black 5' as compared to an Austin Allegro.

It is now approaching 20 years since that melancholy day in August 1968 when normal revenue-earning standard-gauge steam traction hauled the last train on BR metals. BR's attitude to steam has since then completed a somersault. From sneering hostility, through indifference, to bored offhandedness, to faintly amused disdain, to casual interest, to acceptance, now to welcome, we have seen attitudes change in the face of relentless enthusiasm. From the total ban, we arrived at the 1984 summer season of a full and regular steam service again on a BR line, the marvellous West Highland from Fort William to Mallaig. BR management, to their lasting credit, have indeed seen the light on the road to Damascus. Sir Robert Reid, Chairman of BR, talks with enthusiasm of the proposed East Grinstead extension on the Bluebell Railway, and of the Severn Valley Railway and the Kidderminster link. Steam, in the shape of *Sir Nigel Gresley*, returned to Marylebone in 1985.

Talk of Damascus enables me to change the subject and to note the change too in the attitude of some British railway enthusiasts towards foreign steam. Necessity being the mother of invention, those of us seeking the sight, sound and smell of a working steam railway have perforce had no choice but to abandon the shores of our island and seek solace afar. India and China, Poland or Turkey, feature regularly as destinations for 'real' as opposed to 'preserved' railway photography and genuine enjoyment. Damascus indeed provided me with one of my most memorable and enjoyable railway experiences of recent times.

In a book about British steam — and it was incomparably superior to any other — it could be an abuse to dwell too long on foreign matters. However, as leader of an Inter-Parliamentary Union (IPU) delegation to Syria in 1984 I only slightly abused my position by asking to visit the Cadem locomotive works of the Hedjaz Railway in Damascus. It is true that I had happened to mention to the Syrian Ambassador in London, prior to our departure, my passing interest in steam . . . yet, even in my wildest fantasy no place existed for the experience laid on by our Syrian hosts.

Bournemouth shed's rebuilt 'Merchant Navy' 4–6–2 No. 35021 *New Zealand Line* looks in fine fettle heading an up express near Winchester Junction on 14 July 1965. That she was but a month away from withdrawal says all that is necessary about the indecent haste with which steam was eradicated. By October, 35021 was scrapped at Eastleigh Works. Winchester's urban sprawl has engulfed the green fields hereabouts, as electrification turned it into outer surburbia.

I could have chosen any one of dozens of photographs of this jaunty veteran enjoying its final fling in steam, at Cadem, Damascus in March 1984. The brotherhood of steam transcends the differences of creed, colour, politics and personal background, and is encapsulated by this Hartmann 2–6–0T, sprightly in its ninetieth year. She had just completed the 'British Parliamentary Special' as described on page 13: undoubtedly the last steam at Cadem.

To the leader of a Parliamentary delegation falls the responsibility of keeping the team happy and intact. Members of Parliament are by nature individualists, often with strong prejudices and predilections. When, therefore, our Syrian hosts suggested that the delegation might visit the Hedjaz Station in Damascus, after lunch on our third day there, I needed to summon all my tact and persuasive powers lest my colleagues felt either that I was abusing my role as leader, or that our hosts were being too bizarre — or probably a combination of both. The goodwill and camaraderie of Labour and Conservative Members alike was never better illustrated as they succumbed to my blandishment. 'It isn't far from the hotel and will be architecturally worthwhile,' I cajoled. 'As they have asked us to go, and we have an informal afternoon anyway until this evening, just grin and bear it.' With remarkable goodwill and generosity they agreed, and within a few minutes our cavalcade of cars pulled up outside the ornate but diminutive building.

The booking-hall alone merited the journey, with its high, decorative ceiling and inlaid floor. As we imbibed the atmosphere of the place, I was beckoned towards the doorway which led from the hall, out on to the terminus platforms.

My blasphemous exclamation was surely justified. Spurting

vertically upwards in the dry, still air was a cascade of vivid clear white steam. At the platform, proud and immaculate, stood an ancient little tank-engine pulsating with life, and obviously raring to go. Alerted by my exclamation, my Parliamentary colleagues quickly joined me on the platform. What a sight! Our hosts had had put into steam, and immaculately groomed, one of the Swiss-built tank-engines, dating from the 19th century. There she stood attached to a single coach with a balconied open-end: the enthusiasm of my colleagues for the spirit and élan of the little tank-engine was an unspoken eulogy in praise of steam.

There was a 100% turnout of the delegation for the proffered ride through Damascus behind this Victorian gem. I just had time to take some photographs that are undoubtedly unique, historic and unrepeatable. Unquestionably this would be the last-ever steam departure on the narrow-gauge tracks from Damascus Hedjaz Station. The engines had already been withdrawn: the standard-gauge rebuilding programme had already reached the outskirts of the city. Indeed, Russian-built standard gauge diesels soon hove into view, just a few miles from the terminus.

As we trundled through the inner and then the outer suburbs of the Syrian capital, our merry little tank-engine whistled joyously. Never was there a better illustration of the ability of steam to communicate friendship and bonhomie than the response which our cavalcade evoked from those whom we passed. Our journey ended at Cadem. As we approached the site of the works, the graveyard of dead Hedjaz Railway locomotives told its own tale. As my Parliamentary colleagues disembarked from the train and climbed into the waiting cars to take them back to Damascus, I watched our little Swiss engine uncouple her coach and make her way onto the shed. As I followed on foot I felt, strangely, the ghosts of Rose Grove lay their clammy hands on me. As surely as that day in August 1968 when steam finally succumbed on Britain's railways, so I knew in my bones that Cadem would not again see a locomotive drop its fire . . .

I could write at length about that splendid little vintage 1894-built Swiss Hartmann 2–6–0T that trundled jauntily from Hedjaz Station to Cadem; about the ghosts that haunted Cadem's steam graveyard; about the proud redundant old Syrian driver; about the enthusiasm for steam which was evinced by Akil Ismail the Director General of the Hedjaz Railway. So to do would confirm only what you already know; that affection for the steam-engine knows no barriers of colour, class or creed. For anyone whose imagination or memory is captured or indeed captivated by Dai Woodham's graveyard at Barry, a visit to Cadem would undoubtedly evince many a pang, many a painful twinge. For the sight of rusting hulks of what were once live steam engines is a sight that

13

itself tugs at the emotions. It was this, perhaps morbid, lure that pulled me not once but thrice from the beach, sun and sand of our Halkidiki holiday hotel in 1982 to Thessaloniki. In this northern Greek city are three separate dumps of steam-engines, including some built in, and others that once worked in, Britain. Perhaps I should include in this book a chapter entitled 'Corner of a Foreign Field . . .' Yes, I shall. After all, my four previous railway books have all included photographs of dead and derelict engines. *In Praise of Steam* will include memories not only of those engines that I knew and photographed *before* they passed away.

The Greek railway authorities in Thessaloniki, as elsewhere, did their utmost to accommodate my search for steam. (I reject the word 'research' as too pretentious for my inquisitiveness, and in deference to those dedicated souls who really have researched the subject.) Unlike my sojourn in Syria, we were not blessed with almost constant sunshine in Greece. However, that enabled me to persuade my long-suffering wife Jane to allow me to slip away on those three separate occasions. On one of these I managed finally to unearth two oil-fired 'USA' 0–6–0 tank engines kept in working order in Salonika (it's easier to write than Thessaloniki) and to photograph engines once a familiar sight in Southampton Docks, and latterly at Guildford shed. It is the sights and sound, the memories and recollection of British steam that you really hanker after, is it not? Yet surely you will share with me the search for the soul of departed steam, especially if it has some British connection? Thus I sought and eventually found British-built 'Austerity' 2–10–0s as well as the 'USA' tanks. Perhaps the most exciting discovery at Salonika, however, was an ancient 4–4–0 which I now know to have been an American engine built sometime between 1860–1880, and used on Greek metals until 1948. It made a poignant picture.

Railways and politics have become irretrievably entwined in my life, so perhaps I can jump from Greece to Cyprus, in railway terms, without too much difficulty, although it is to Northern (Turkish) Cyprus that I next make passing reference. At the time of writing this Introduction, my preliminary research has revealed very little about the Cyprus railway system, save only that it was narrow gauge, not very extensive, and that it closed in 1951. Information aplenty followed my acquisition of *The Story of the Cyprus Government Railway* by Lieutenant Colonel B. S. Turner.

In Famagusta, mounted on a plinth beside the old station building, stands a dimunitive Hunslet 0–6–0 tank engine, lovingly maintained in good external order by someone who cares, following restoration in 48 Command workshop REME in June 1972. It bears proudly its manufacturer's plate 'The Hunslet

Engineering Co Ltd Leeds No 846–1904'. A stone tablet bears the information that the delightful locomotive was the first to be imported into Cyprus, was used during the construction period of the Government Railway and thereafter in its operation from 1904 to 1951. (See page 153.)

The Colonial Administration in Cyprus, in its annual publication for 1903, included the following paragraph: 'There are no railways or tramways in Cyprus. A survey was made by Lieut Pritchard, RE in 1899, for a railway from Nicosia to Famagusta, the cost of which he estimated at £130,000; and for one from Nicosia to Larnaca, the cost of which he estimated at £47,000. The construction of a line of 2ft 6in gauge, from Famagusta through Nicosia towards Caravostasi, at a cost of about £140,000 is to begin in the spring of 1904. Resident Engineer (on behalf of Messrs Shelford & Son, Consulting Engineers to the Crown Agents), G. B. Day.'

Cyprus yielded two more narrow-gauge locomotives to my inquisitive camera. One of them lay seemingly undiscovered and unknown to our Cypriot friends until my persistent inquisitiveness unearthed it among the industrial dereliction of the Cyprus Mining Corporation's former arena of activity at Xeros. However, it was an ugly American narrow-gauge machine, although its manufacturer's plate is a pleasing trophy. I am anxious, though, to return to writing about railways that properly require only two adjectives to legitimise them: 'British' and 'standard-gauge'. In truth, one could write extensively about Belgian locomotives in Jordan, American locomotives in Turkey, German locomotives in Greece or Swiss locomotives in Syria, to name but four. I have written a book called *To China for Steam*, which speaks for itself. But it is regular, revenue-earning, British-built engines, at work in their declining years between 1962 and 1968, on LMS, LNER, SR and, of course, GWR territory, that is my predominant task here.

The attraction of the railway as a subject is hard to define, but includes among its attributes strong elements of human interest and of our nation's history. Notwithstanding the increased interest in foreign railways concomitant with the demise of steam on Britain's railways, the majority of my native fellow railway enthusiasts remain, in spite of ourselves, nationalistic in our proclivities. This phenomenon manifests itself in both the continuing stream of books on our railways in the steam era; and the very nature of these books, which have undergone and continue to undergo a subtle, but marked transformation. Thus we see published books comprising immense detail of the history, geography and operation of selected stretches of line. We find biographies of drivers, firemen, signalmen from the steam era;

Maunsell's 'N' and 'U' Class Moguls were a familiar sight for around forty years on both main and secondary lines of the Southern Railway and its successor. By 1965, however, their days were clearly numbered. The first weekend of the year was their last on one of their remaining passenger strongholds, the Reading–Redhill trains on the former SECR line. Saturday 2 January dawned crisp and sunny: a perfect winter's day. With the aid of my Guildford shed pass I obtained a strategic photographic location, perhaps to the annoyance of others who had come to record the end of an era. Unlike most of the SECR line, the immediate area around Guildford was third-rail country, as is evident from this shot of 'U' No. 31627 blasting out of the station with the 13.35 Redhill to Reading train. These locomotives were the epitome of reliability and versatility.

and we find books of photographs covering railway ephemera from clocks to uniforms, goods wagons to station buildings. Surprisingly, there seems still to be an extensive supply of black-and-white photographs, many previously unpublished, emerging from the trunks and attics of those who lived in the steam era, but whose earthly span has reached the terminus in the sky. Not all the photographic records maintain the highest standards – and that certainly includes the efforts of this pedestrian practitioner, who is painfully aware that his efforts with the camera are published by virtue of the shortage of contemporary colour material, rather than of artistic merit or photographic talent.

At this stage of writing my 'Introduction' I rely on an 'engineered accident' of meeting a railwayman from the steam era. By oozing into the cab of a diesel or electric BR locomotive there is still the likelihood of finding oneself in the company of 'a man of steam'. As an outspoken pro-railway Parliamentarian, my friends in BR management are always willing to satisfy my requests in this direction, although an unofficial request to an unprepared driver is invariably more rewarding than a pre-arranged cab-ride accompanied by an inspector. Human nature inevitably plays a part, and a driver who has volunteered to share his cab with an enthusiast makes a less inhibited companion than a driver accompanied by 'officialdom'. However, I digress, because of my three reminiscences this time, two comprised 'official' footplate journeys, and one was with a bus man, not a railwayman. (I was tempted to put an exclamation mark, rather than a full stop, at the end of that last sentence, but decided against so doing. There seems to be an overwhelming temptation confronting reminiscing railway authors, liberally to use this form of punctuation, to the point of exasperation to me as a reader and presumably to others, so I aim to avoid the temptation.) Neither of the footplate journeys, however, was an ordinary event. The first was in the cab of the Advanced Passenger Train (APT) on which I was BR's guest on a special Euston to Glasgow Central run on 26 September 1984. Here I met James Lake, to whom I referred earlier; yet another hero, another man of steam, who will now have retired from a lifetime of dedicated service to the railway. But, even in the cab of Britain's most prestigious railway project – for in spite of its trials and tribulations it remains just that, notwithstanding our national obsession with self-denigration – it was his memories of the past, rather than his description of the present, that caused James Lake's eyes to sparkle.

Few people fail to enjoy the chance to reminisce with Prime Ministers, hobnob with Royalty or ogle stars of stage or screen. For me, however, the opportunity to listen to the measured tones

James Lake, senior driver at Euston, alongside the cab of the Advanced Passenger Train (APT) on the occasion of its run from Euston to Glasgow Central on 26 September 1984. Starved of adequate funds of cash by government or – equally important – of senior management commitment and enthusiasm, APT has still not yet fulfilled its potential. James Lake is proud of his APT, but makes no bones about the missing camaraderie that disappeared with steam.

of a former top link engine driver, far surpasses the pleasures of chatting with the famous, the important or the glamorous. At the time of our meeting, Lake was senior driver at Euston. Yet even this august position seemed to him less rewarding than his recollection of joining the LMS at Camden in 1937. As he spoke of the camaraderie of those pre-war days, he made no bones about his views on the inter-relationship of management and men in the steam era. As he said, 'The chief mechanical engineer knew that however fine his design, however special his new development, it was ultimately the ability of the fireman and driver to harness their skill and effort to his design that determined success or failure.'

How many modern engineers, he mused, take the trouble to meet the drivers of today's diesel and electric engines? Of course, he acknowledged that cleanliness has replaced the unremitting grime of steam – but he summed it up thus – 'Cleanliness has replaced camaraderie,' and in the modern railway, he felt that 'teamwork had gone out of management'.

As he explained the intricacies of his 'dashboard', with its relayed information from track to cab through transponders, our APT ran through Weaver Junction and James Lake began again to recall his memories of the end of the steam era. Still a Camden man, he saw out his final years as a senior steam driver 'on the Manchesters and Liverpools'. Naturally, as an LMS man, he gave the highest marks to the 'Coronations'.

As we approached Warrington my memory recalled a shot I took in July 1965 at the long-abandoned Fidlers Ferry & Penketh Station, between Warrington and Widnes, of an Ivatt 'Flying Pig', trundling light engine past the weed-strewn, overgrown platform. I fell silent as we sped through Bank Quay Station. As we passed the site of Dallam Shed, I shared with my cab-companion memories of the closing years of steam, hereabouts. How grateful I am both to Ian Allan and Blandford Press, whose publishing divisions have enabled me to embalm in perpetuity some of my most treasured photographic memories. Grey, gloomy winter days heightened rather than diminished the atmosphere of places like Warrington with its extensive railway environment. As I soliloquised to the APTs cab occupants about '4F's, '8F's, 'Jubilee's, 'Black 5's and 'Britannia's, still plentiful and hard at work in late 1964, less than 20 years prior to our conversation, I was gripped by that intense sadness, longing and nostalgia for those declining days of steam. They are gone, for ever. For me nothing can replace the feeling of anticipation as one clicked the shutter on a scene that one knew, beyond peradventure, would soon be but a memory. If one could live on memories, even I, a late, late starter on the stage of steam era railway photography, could survive until eternity. How grateful I remain to my wife Jane for galvanizing me to an 'outdoor activity' at the end of 1962, and which resulted in nearly six glorious years of chasing steam around Britain.

It was the last Friday of the 1984 Summer Recess when I kept my afternoon appointment in Poole with Allan Rolls, General Manager of the Wilts & Dorset Bus Company. Pouring rain, strong wind, inaccurate instructions and an aggravated back (caused by trying to move the level-crossing gate-opening wheel in my garage) saw me in an unattractive mood as I finally reached his office. Rarely however has my complexion changed so quickly in meteorological terms from 'stormy' to 'set fair' than it did that afternoon. Before we had had time even to exchange formal greetings, I saw copies of *In Search of Steam*, *Call of Steam* and *To China for Steam* sitting on his table. We started talking steam immediately.

Allan Rolls' grandfather, Ernest Rolls, had been a Southern driver, based at Bournemouth Shed. He it was who took young Allan down to the depot where he succumbed instantly to the lure of the steam engine. Another enthusiast was enrolled into the 'Brotherhood of Steam'.

Without apologising for including another Southern locomotive in this Introduction, Eastleigh's Rebuilt 'Battle of Britain' 4–6–2 No. 34088 *213 Squadron*, devoid of nameplate, moves out of Guildford Station, light engine, on 2 January 1965. Built post-Nationalisation in BR days, 34088 had 9 ft wide cab and tender, the latter carrying 5,500 gallons of water as opposed to the 4,500 gallons of the earlier members of the class. This engine was sometimes used on State occasions, such as the visit of the King and Queen of Greece on 9 July 1963. She was withdrawn in March 1967, stored at Nine Elms and then at Salisbury until February 1968, whence she departed for her final destination, Cashmores of Newport, where she was cut up in the following month.

Instead of 'interviewing' a railwayman, I thought I might 'interview' a fellow-enthusiast. Allan Rolls was eight when he 'joined the club'. As though it were yesterday, he began to recall those days, some 40 years ago, when he first started 'spotting'. Old Ernest's last engine, in those final years of the SR, was No. 865, one of the 'Lord Nelson' class of express passenger 4–6–0 locomotives. Allan started to talk, and as I listened, I envied him.

'He used to take me on the footplate, and soon my visits were almost a daily occurrence. Sometimes he, or one of his fellow-drivers, would let me ride on the footplate about the yard. Then, again, my mother and I would go to Bournemouth Central Station, and I would be smuggled on to the footplate, whilst she travelled in the front carriage of the Bournemouth–Weymouth train as far as Poole. There we both got off – me off the footplate and she off the train. We then went into Poole Park and spent time there, or in the town, until grandfather came back with the train from Weymouth. Again I would be taken on to the footplate, whilst she rode in the front carriage back to Bournemouth.'

I did not cross-examine Allan about the type of locomotive or its performance up Parkstone Bank. This was towards the end of the war. By 1946/7, grandfather Ernest had graduated to that final steed, No. 865 *Sir John Hawkins* – 'that was his engine'. Again I scribbled furiously as Allan Rolls reminisced. 'He sparkled, his engine sparkled, as they all did. Grandmother sent him off to work every day with clean overalls and, of course, with clean boots . . .'

In Allan Rolls I found a near-contemporary enthusiast, although I could not boast a grandfather as an engine-driver. The waxing and waning of his enthusiasm sounded the echoes of my own. His grandfather retired in 1948, but Allan's spotting activities continued. At about the age of 13 he began to show an interest in aircraft. Railway interest faded and lay dormant until 1963. Then, being transferred from Hants & Dorset to Thames Valley Bus Company he was sent to Reading, where he found himself working for a bus company seemingly staffed with railway enthusiasts. He emerged from his long hibernation of disinterest, with lunch-time visits to both Reading South (SR) and Reading Great Western sheds. 'I recall waiting for the 1.10 Paddington to Worcester and Hereford, and realising they were the last regular express trains ever to be hauled by "Castles".' Don't we all . . .

From 1963–1965 he saw steam dying on the GWR at Reading. Thereafter he was transferred away to Norwich, where dieselisation (a word as ugly as the machine) had arrived. 'Then it was books, and slowly, perhaps unawares, there grew an interest in

Commuting from Sunningdale to Waterloo enabled me occasionally to capture a shot of the morning westbound freight from Feltham, or even, as on 16 May 1964, the locomotive shunting the yard at Staines Central. Fellow-travellers, with faces buried in the *Financial Times*, seldom appreciated my insistence on opening the window and leaning out with camera poised. Southern motive power varied from 'S15's, through Bulleid Light Pacifics, occasionally a 'W' tank, as well as the 'Q1' 0–6–0, of which class Feltham's No. 33026 was performing on this day. As is evident here, moving trains rarely provided the ideal platform for colour photography in the steam era, when 1000 ASA colour film was an unimagined dream. 33026 was one of the last survivors of a distinctively ugly but efficient class, bearing the unmistakeable hallmark of O.V.S. Bulleid.

Notice the lattice signal-post and finial, part of the departed charm of the steam era.

overseas steam. Now I'm a good customer,' he said, indicating *To China for Steam*.

Railway enthusiasm is a hobby, an interest, almost a disease. As addicts whose specific drug supply – steam – diminished and finally disappeared in 1968, some turned to preservation, some to books, some to overseas steam. For our spouses our obsession can sometimes go too far. Although modelling holds no interest for me, probably because of my ineptitude at *making* things, my particular penchant has become *collecting* things: usually dirty, heavy, metal objects from the steam era, but including items of signalling equipment and so forth. Yet still there burns that urge to record photographically a steam era that is nearing the nadir of its existence, even in China where, at Datong, steam engines are still being built.

Over the years, the creation of opportunities to escape from official or family commitments has itself become something of a specialised exercise. My successful 'achievements' have included a number of overseas 'events', some of which are listed.

Occasion	Venue Intended	Escape Location
Parliamentary Delegation (People's Republic of China)	Great Wall of China	Nan Kou Locomotive Works
Parliamentary Delegation (Syria)	Damascus Souk	Cadem Locomotive Works
Monaco Grand Prix	Monte Carlo	Nice Engine Shed
Family Holiday – beach	Halkidiki, Greece	Salonika Engine Dumps
British–Swiss Ski-ing Event	Davos	Landquart Motive Power Depot
Parliamentary Fact-Finding Visit	Northern Cyprus	Cyprus Mining – Derelict Railway
Parliamentary Delegation (Jordan)	Amman Airport	Amman Engine Shed

This is just a sample. Not included are the innumerable instances of truancy, from the age of four, to date, encompassing the purloining of time more properly devoted to educational or commercial activity, mainly in Britain, the range, extent and frequency of which doubtless partly account for my ignorance and poverty.

Naturally steam has been the object of the chase. Just occasionally, however, one's interest is titillated by rolling stock or by other forms of motive power. The most recent of the latter was at Landquart MPD in Switzerland. My target was the two preserved 2–8–0's owned and operated by the Rhätische Bahn, and shedded at Landquart. Being early January I failed to plead, bluster or cajole Walter Frech into moving the locomotives from their winter quarters in their shed, out on to the turntable. However, my eye was smitten by a venerable electric shunter. Built in 1913 it is a mere seven years younger than the two Schweitzerische Locomotiv & Maschinenfabrik 2–8–0's. Immaculate in dark brown livery, I persuaded Walter Frech, with assistance, to start up the 2–4–2 shunter and bring her out of the shed on to the Landquart turntable. Still retained as a standby shunter, this veteran has already served the railway for more than 72 years, and is expected to be retained for some time to come. Could it be the oldest electric locomotive still in regular service anywhere in the world?

So, dear reader, welcome to this, my fifth railway book, and my fourth on British steam. My collection of photographs taken between November 1962 and August 1968, has far outstripped the potential I imagined it possessed, when my first book, *British Steam in Camera Colour*, was published in 1979. It has been my good fortune to find publishers who enable me to write my rambling reminiscences to match my amateur snapshots. Techniques of colour printing seem now able to make even badly-taken photographs into reasonable pictures. In truth, of course, it is *what* I photographed, not *how* I did so, that has been my good fortune. I knew not the meaning of 'grain', which seems almost to enable me to claim talent for what in reality is ignorance.

A sad note permeates this book. With the untimely death of Derek Cross, Britain has lost one of the finest railway photographers. Derek, like the steam engine, was larger than life, ebullient, enthusiastic and mischievously irascible. Wit and raconteur of railway lore, he had edited, inspected and pungently commented on my previous books of British steam photography. Indeed, his comments were not only amusing in their style, they were pertinent and accurate. Undoubtedly they saved me from some of the more glaring errors that would have disfigured my text and annoyed perspicacious and rightly pernickety enthusiasts. Without Derek, the railway scene is poorer and this book less accurate. I mourn him on both counts. My thanks however to Brian Haresnape for his willingness to subject himself to reading my text.

Jane has always told me – 'choose the photographs and write around them, not vice versa.' This is her polite way of telling me that being with a camera in the right place at the right time, was and is a better adjunct to creating a good railway book, than the 'skill' of my pen. It matters little: my love of the steam-engine, shared by so many, can be reflected in many ways: steam survives eternally in our memory. I come to praise steam, not to bury it.

As 1984 slunk away, and for the Jeremiahs failed dismally to fulfil Orwell's expectations of Armageddon, 1985 came forth, like 1963, in cold, gloom and snow. One's memory inevitably drew comparison with the last great snow-freeze of the steam era, the winter of 1962/3. Exercising my role as joint chairman of the All Party Railways Group at Westminster, I had suggested to Sir

Robert Reid, Chairman of BR, that he might arrange a demonstration run of the 'Sprinter' d.m.u. To this he readily agreed and thus the party of MPs duly collected at St Pancras on the morning of Wednesday 16 January 1985.

It was arranged that we should travel by 'Sprinter' to Luton and back. Luton. Immediately my mind flashed to November 1962, my only previous sojourn on railway property at a place more renowned for the dreaded internal combustion engine than for steam, or special railway interest. On that dull, grey, damp day some 22 years previously, I had managed but two photographs; of an '8F' plodding through the station on a southbound freight; and of a Fairburn 2–6–4T pausing briefly, light engine, in what my records now quaintly call 'Luton Midland Road'. Numbered 48467 and 42086 respectively, they have escaped inclusion in previous books, and only at the instant of writing these words have I had cause to refer to 'the gospel according to Peter Hands' – in other words 'What Happened To Steam' – to check the whereabouts of these two engines.

According to Hands, 42086 was based at Cricklewood (14A) from June 1962. That would tally with a presence at Luton. I cast my eye over her later years. September 1964, transferred to 8H Birkenhead! Could it possibly be that I saw 42086 in her declining years. Frantically scouring my faithful record book, with feverish anticipation . . . Surely my luck would not . . . yes, there it is . . . X32 'Simmering outside shed: 42782 + 48522 + 42086: 4 September 1965.' Excuse my childish thrill at such a discovery. What about 48467? I write these words before looking into Hands, volume 28. 48467. December 1962. 15B Kettering. That's reasonable for Luton. Where thereafter? 15E, Coalville. 15A, Leicester Midland. Never got to either shed. Then 8A: Edge Hill. Ah, I was there, later. Then 9H: Patricroft – put down pencil . . . 48674 at Speke Junction. 48476 there, too, and at Lostock Hall. 48764 at Lostock Hall: 48471 at Manchester Victoria: 48423 at Rose Grove: 48167 at Carnforth; it seems that this 'double' has eluded me. If only that computer program actually worked, then not only would cross-checking numbers be simple, who knows what coincidences of multiple-sightings it might reveal?

All this soliloquy emanates from my ruminations at St Pancras as we prepared to board the 'Sprinter' to Luton. Let us return. With my colleagues Robert Hicks, David Mudd, Colin Shepherd, Conal Gregory, John Marek and others, we boarded unit 150 001 on Platform 7. Naturally I sought the opportunity to ride in the cab, and my BR friends, as ever, obliged. As we accelerated smartly away from the Midland Railway's London terminus, I was introduced to the driver, Ralph Moore, and Traction Inspector Roy Shephard. Both Derby men, they were condemned to listen to my inconsequential reminiscences of steam days at St Pancras, which were mercifully – for their sake – few, but included one of my first colour railway photographs, of a 'Jubilee' departing on a Leeds express, at the end of 1962.

As usual, having exchanged polite comment and expressed the requisite interest in yet another doubtless efficient but undoubtedly characterless form of BR motive power, I began to pump my new 'recruits' for their reminiscences of the steam era. Ralph Moore joined the LMS at Derby Shed, as a cleaner, in 1947. By the end of the steam era he was a passed fireman. Of the engines he fired and drove, and on which he worked at Derby, he was precise and unequivocal: 'the Black Five was the best; no doubt about it'. Perhaps he was somewhat less intent to sing the praise of steam than was Roy Shephard, from whom the memories came tumbling forth. As we sped north through Harpenden he reminisced about his years following his joining the LMS in 1941. He had spent some time at Nottingham, and then at Kirkby in Ashfield, which shed closed, as 16E, in October 1966. 'You had to run your fire down uphill, which ever way you went at it,' he mused.

We talked of matters LMS, and Roy mentioned that 'William Michael Stanier – the great man's grandson – is with us at Derby, right now. He's at Nelson Street; CME at HQ.'

A propos of nothing in particular save the magic of association with the great names of the world of steam, it was through sheer inquisitiveness I looked up a few names in the Uppingham School Roll. There is no 'Stanier', but what of 'Gresley'? Gresley, Roger (L), b. July 1906; s. of Sir N. Gresley, CBE, DSc, Doncaster.

Stanier, Gresley: we honour and praise them, their achievements. They have their memorials, in deed and word. As a pedestrian scribbler of railway reminiscences, the mere mention of such names, of Churchward and Collett, Maunsell and Bulleid, brings a glow, a memory perhaps by inference attributable to James Watt. *In Praise of Steam*.

1 Eastern Approaches

The time-honoured conundrum featuring the chicken and the egg is reflected each time I sit down to write a new railway book. As already mentioned, it manifests itself in the soliloquised question 'shall I write my chapters and find the photographs to fit, or shall I select my transparencies and then do the writing?' Inevitably one compromises as no great issue of principle is involved. Ultimately it is the chapter-titles as much as anything, that determine the outcome, and the avoidance of repetition becomes an important criterion. Herein lies the rub.

The fact that almost every common adjective has been attached to the word 'steam' and almost every evocative phrase utilised in designating railway book titles, stretches our imagination. Fortunately my books, being anecdotes and personal reminiscences attached to my own photographs, enable me to escape into the realms, if not of fantasy then certainly beyond the necessarily stereotyped and predictable, when choosing chapter-headings. My gambler's instincts, inherited from my maternal grandfather, come into play, and goad me into choosing subjects where my photographic supply is limited. In *The Call of Steam* I gambled on 'Yorkshire' and 'Midlands': this time it is this chapter that sees my photo-collection spread most thin, and – as is self-evident – sees me scraping my photographic barrel.

Undoubtedly the lines of the LNER were those that I covered least in my increasingly frantic search for steam in its declining years. Whilst GWR and SR territory were the nearest to home, it was the LMS in the North-West that saw out the end of steam and, not coincidentally, was the area of proximity to much of my time spent on commercial and political duty. Indeed, the juxtaposition of my personal geography and steam's earlier demise on LNER lines than elsewhere, created its own situation for me and accounts for my paucity of material. In asking you, therefore, to excuse the rambling opening to this chapter, you will nevertheless deduce herefrom the fact that lack of opportunity rather than conscious prejudice occasions an apparent imbalance in the regional selection of the photographs in this book.

Perhaps for the record, too, I should repeat a point made in earlier books, concerning my use of railway language. I abhor the prefix 'ex' when describing locomotives. A 'Castle' as far as I am concerned is a GWR engine; likewise a 'Black 5' is LMS, a 'Schools' is SR and you will not find, and I trust not mind, my rejecting the phrase 'ex-LNER' to describe, say a 'B1'. With the pre-grouping classes too my adjectival designation is usually related to the parentage rather than to subsequent ownership. Thus an 'M7' is an LSWR engine, and so forth. Obviously all the Riddles-imprinted Standard classes are designed 'BR'. That is my style, for which no apology is offered.

Now let me return to 'Eastern Approaches'. With my faithful catalogue by my side, it is apparent how limited was my coverage of LNER territory, although happily my first month of adventure as re-born railway enthusiast, with camera, November 1962, saw me at King's Cross. Indeed, that first foray was occasioned by elucidating the information that the Eastern Region was to be the first to eliminate steam from London. Class 'A2/3' Pacific No. 60523 *Sun Castle*, photographed backing out of the terminus and heading for Top Shed was amongst the first of my colour photographs. That experience at King's Cross determined me to gain entrance to Top Shed. It was three months before ambition was fulfilled, by which time steam was facing extinction.

Those first few weeks of my photographic 'career' were very much a time of 'hit and miss' photography, mainly from station platforms; and in terms of reproducible results, more 'miss' than 'hit' seems to have been the outcome. My determination and lack of inhibition soon gained me access to more exciting places; yet the only LNER engines I photographed between November 1962 and my visit to Top Shed in March 1963, were 'A3' 4–6–2 No. 60071 *Tranquil* with German smoke-deflectors and 'V2' 2–6–2 No. 60906, travelling at speed through Welwyn Garden City Station, on express fitted freights. It was a cold, murky February afternoon with snow on the ground. Even if I had known, then, what 'grain' meant and if today's fast colour film had been invented, and if I had had a modern camera, it is doubtful whether the end-product would have been much less dismal, late that winter afternoon.

There is a bitter-sweet melancholy morbidity in looking through my catalogue-book of those first few months. Inevitably we are creatures of our own environment. My photographs act as a pictorial diary in recording my movements. Bristol: Luton: Olympia: Paddington: Highbridge: 'North of St Albans':

It must have been the first or the last on the film in my camera that caused me to take this shot. The modern fashion for photographing close-up detail had not yet become the done thing. However, bright sunshine on the brass plate on the cabside of Gresley 'A3' 4–6–2 No. 60063 *Isinglass* at Top Shed in March 1963 appealed to me – as can be seen. I have never made the slightest attempt to pretend that Gresley's 'A4's thrilled me. For me, his 'A3' Pacifics were the pinnacle of the elegance for which his reputation will endure. Thompson mangled them, Peppercorn updated them, but the 'A3's were the true thoroughbreds – as they were rightly named. *Isinglass* was fitted with German-style smoke-deflectors as late as August 1961, even though the first 'A3' was withdrawn at the end of 1959. I wonder where this plate is, or if it survived.

Weston-super-Mare: Queens Road Battersea: Vauxhall: St Pancras: Hove: all record the odd snatched moments of weekend visits to family in Somerset and Sussex, plus sloping-off from Jane at weekends when we lived in our first home in Chiswick. It is only a matter of time, however, before the magic initials 'MPD' begin to appear in the catalogue. Yet still, in spite of the mobility afforded by my job, there is a significant lack of 'Eastern promise'.

March 1963 brought a visit to Manchester, as Sales Director of the May Fair Hotel (two words, in those days) without yet the realisation of Manchester's steam-photography potential. My hobby had yet to become the obsession into which it matured as steam diminished rapidly. By the time I had come fully to appreciate Manchester, in 1964, LNER steam thereabouts was almost extinct. A fleeting visit to Manchester Central, late at night, enabled me to photograph 'B1' 4–6–0 No. 61369 at about 11 p.m. At this early period of my photography, detailing precise information did not seem so vital as it in fact was – and is – to satisfy myself and anyone else interested. There was, of course, no thought whatsoever in my mind that any of my transparencies might end up being published. By this date *Railway Observer*, the invaluable monthly magazine of the Railway Correspondence and Travel Society (RCTS) was reporting Great Central information under London Midland Region, for the Manchester area, to which it had been transferred.

This book, like its predecessors, owes much to *Railway Observer*, to which I pay fulsome praise and give inestimable thanks. The May 1964 issue records another 'B1', No. 61275, as having rescued an ailing 'Black 5' on the overnight Manchester to Marylebone sleeper, on 21 March that year. The same issue incidentally records the end of the Uppingham School Specials: an odd coincidence as I write these words the day following my return from acting as Chairman of the Quadringenary Dinner which ended the celebration of the 400th anniversary of my old school, and which prompted the glance through the Uppingham School Roll to which I referred at the end of my Introduction.

Perhaps we should return to the LNER. On 28 March 1963 business took me to Leeds. A mere five minutes at Leeds City Station was all I could manage. It was raining: of the two photographs taken, one was of 'A1' 4–6–2 No. 60155 *Borderer* receiving final attention from the driver prior to departure: the other, of Fowler 2–6–4T No. 42409 shunting vans. Sadly my camera was loaded with Gevacolour film, the quality of which was so inferior to Kodachrome that I soon learned not to use it. Gevacolour shots had faded within 10 years or less, whilst Kodak's products still maintain their colour 20 or more years after exposure.

As I thumb through my catalogue in search of LNER steam, my next entry brings me to 18 May 1963, but the locations are hardly on LNER territory. On that date, *Flying Scotsman* headed a Gainsborough Model Railway Society special from Lincoln to Eastleigh. I caught the famous 'A3' at Basingstoke, and then photographed her at Eastleigh, alongside an LSWR 'M7' 0–4–4T, still in BR service. My first genuine 'Eastern' sighting, excepting King's Cross and Top Shed, occurred on 20 July 1963, when I managed to visit Peterborough New England shed. By this date the 'A4's had departed Top Shed for ever, and New England shed was their southern outpost although Peterborough 'A4's still worked to King's Cross. No. 60007 *Sir Nigel Gresley* was on shed, together with 60017 *Silver Fox* and 60034 *Lord Faringdon*. I captured them for posterity, together with 'B1' No. 61207, the latter just five months before withdrawal. Also dead on shed and photographed was 'A2/3' 4–6–2 No. 60523 – my friend *Sun Castle*: and 'O1' 2–8–0 No. 63872. Little did I imagine that I should see *Sir Nigel Gresley* at Marylebone more than 21 years later.

The pre-grouping eight-coupled heavy freight locomotives, some of which survived to a ripe old age, largely eluded me. I

Sun Castle awaits her fate. First photographed at King's Cross in November 1962 (*British Steam in Camera Colour*): then running light engine to Top Shed some four months later (*Call of Steam*): 'A2/3' No. 60523 had dropped her fire for the last time when I found her soon after withdrawal amidst a long line of other discarded engines at New England shed, Peterborough on 7 July 1963. She was in fact cut up at Doncaster Works the following month. Like the memory of Qin Shi Huang, I shall always remember *Sun Castle*.

always envied those able to see the splendid Raven North Eastern 'Q6' and 'Q7' 0–8–0's, but of course there were none down at Peterborough. However, I did also manage to grab a shot of Gresley 'A3', No. 60085 *Manna*, which class to me far outshone his 'A4s' in style and shape. *Manna* in fact had had those controversial smoke deflectors fitted as recently as April 1962. Based at Gateshead in June 1963 she was withdrawn from there in October 1964, and was finally cut up by Drapers at Hull, in January 1965. For all this detailed information, I am indebted, as are many others, to Peter Hands, whose series 'What Happened to Steam?' is an astonishing labour of love, invaluable to the dedicated enthusiast.

On 4 February 1964, I managed to pay my one and only visit to genuine Great Eastern territory. I cannot actually remember how I came to be in March that day, but even my stranger's eyes could see that it was but a pale shadow of the place it must once have been. Of the locomotives I photographed – a day of rather flat light, sadly – only four were genuine LNER engines: 'B1' 4–6–0's numbers 61143/318/23, and Frodingham (36C) 'O4/8' 2–8–0 No. 63653. '8F' and 'WD' 2–8–0's, plus '9F' 2–10–0s reminded me that once this place must have been a mecca for recording 'foreign' freight engines.

My greatest regret is never to have seen in action those splendid North Eastern 'Q6' or 'Q7' 0–8–0's, or even the Bowen-Cooke LNWR locomotives, some of which survived almost to the end of steam. Somehow I managed to visit March on 4 February 1964, and was rewarded at least with an eight-coupled LNER locomotive, with pre-grouping ancestry. 'O4/8' 2–8–0 No. 63653, with its 100A boiler, had lost most of its 'Great Central' looks, although unlike the 'O1's it was still only classified '7F'. The cylinders are original. Thompson's plan to rebuild the large stud of Great Central 'O4' class 2–8–0's to Class 'O1' never materialised due to his retirement. For many years a Frodingham engine, where she was still allocated when this (overexposed) shot was taken at March, 63653 was transferred to Doncaster in September 1965, where she became one of the last four survivors, all based there, on withdrawal in April 1966.

From whatever else I did that day, my employer received scant benefit, as my faithful catalogue records visits also to Cambridge and Hitchin. LNER motive power was nowhere in sight at the former, which yielded only 'Black 5' 4–6–0 No. 45089, at that date allocated to Woodford Halse, of formerly Great Central and subsequently LNER heritage. (For the decline and fall of Woodford, see *The Call of Steam*.)

Hitchin, where I arrived in late afternoon, was a sorry sight, and clearly this former Great Northern junction was busily eradicating the memory of steam. However, 'B1' 4–6–0 No. 61109 was in productive employment, albeit an unwilling assistant in the demise of steam hereabouts. She had been transferred finally from Canklow to Peterborough in November '63 and was withdrawn in July '64.

Railway Observer for April 1964 contains a morbid paragraph on Hitchin that says it all, describing the removal of track and facilities, impending demolition of the coaling plant and then the following sentence – 'The C & W building has been razed to the ground and parts of the shed building have been demolished.' Happy days!

At the beginning of April I managed another brief visit to Manchester Central, but this time there was not an LNER loco in sight, the only steam in evidence being one Stanier and one Fairburn 2–6–4T. I was, however, fortunate enough to see another 'B1' on 27 June 1964, albeit well off the beaten track. No. 61327, a Canklow engine, had worked through to Bristol, and was on shed that day at Barrow Road m.p.d. Indeed, there were GWR and BR locomotives there, as well as numerous LMS engines – but that is another story. 61327 was due to work train IV48 from Paignton, forward to Leeds.

By December 1964 I had really 'discovered' Manchester, and had also discovered that that much-maligned area obtains its fair share of sunshine, too. Indeed 3 December was a magnificent sunny winter's day and 'B1' No. 61012 *Puku* made a superb sight as she hurried past Newton Heath carriage sidings on an empty stock train. The photograph was subsequently utilised as one of the series of fifteen postcards produced from my collection by J. Arthur Dixon, so does not qualify for inclusion in this book of previously-unpublished pictures.

By August 1965 I was devoting ever more time to railway photography, but having to tailor my travelling to those areas where limited 'time off' would bring most reward. This meant the North-West, but a planned trip to Edinburgh gave me an overnight stop at Newcastle. How I regret not being less diligent! No time at all was available for shed visits and my photography was limited to shots at Newcastle Central Station, and from the

train window en route to Edinburgh. My memory of the occasion is bright, but the photography less so, although I was certainly able to record some new classes. If only my camerawork was better – but there it is. I captured 'J27' 0–6–0 No. 65805 through my lens, but almost straight into the sun, perforce. However, an elderly North Eastern engine was an exciting capture, to be trumped only by hasty but prized shots – not for the result but for the memory – of two 'Q6' 0–8–0's, Nos. 63366 and 63459. Unfamiliarity with the terrain combined with the speed of the train in which I was travelling, not only marred my photography, but also precluded me from identifying my precise whereabouts. However, thanks to the estimable Peter Hands and 'What Happened to Steam?' I can at least add to the sum of my limited knowledge by recording that, at that time, 63366 was based at Tyne Dock (52H) and 63459 at North Blyth (52F). How satisfying it is, 20 years after one took the photographs, to be able to identify, add to or confirm one's knowledge and information.

That day, after arrival at Edinburgh, was the highlight of my career as a photographer of Eastern steam. I managed to gain entry to St Margarets Shed, and was indeed well rewarded. My previous books have contained a goodly number of the LNER locomotives on shed that afternoon. With the exception of a

Notwithstanding my attempts here to portray the less glamorous side of that railway, a chapter on the heritage of the LNER between 1962 and 1968 would be considered incomplete without featuring an 'A4' and a 'V2'. On my visit to St Margarets shed, Edinburgh, on 5 August 1965, I was able to capture two for the price of one. No. 60027 *Merlin* had been transferred to the shed from Glasgow (St Rollox) in September 1964. Just a year after this photograph she was withdrawn, stored at St Margarets, and scrapped at Campbells, Shieldhall, in February 1966. The 'V2' is No. 60835, which bore one of the longest names impaled on any British locomotive – *The Green Howard, Alexandra, Princess of Wales's Own Yorkshire Regiment*. The nameplate has already disappeared by this date. Only eight of the 184 engines were named. With Gresley's 6' 2" wheel diameter as on his 'P2' 2–8–2's, and a shortened version of the Standard 'A3' boiler, the 'V2' was an outstandingly successful and sure-footed locomotive, even by Gresley's standards. No. 60835, photographed here at her home shed, was fitted with outside steam-pipes. She was withdrawn just three months after this photograph was taken.

Note the piles of ash, just a part of the inevitable dirt of the steam shed. The site is now an office block.

BR/Standard Class '4' 2–6–4T and an LMS Fairburn locomotive of the same wheel arrangement, it was LNER all the way. Perhaps the gem was the shed's stationary boiler, namely North British 'J36' 0–6–0 No. 65234. (See page 95.) From a class introduced in 1888 by Holmes, she stood proud in the summer sun: what a compliment to the design that my Ian Allan *ABC* 'Winter 1962/63 Edition' – before they removed the dates therefrom! – still listed 56 locomotives of a class, even then, about 75 years old. Perhaps your appetite may be whetted by my listing LNER engines photographed on what was, for me, truly a memorable occasion:

A4		A3	
60027	*Merlin*	60041	*Salmon Trout*

V2	
60835	*The Green Howard, Alexandra,*
	Princess of Wales's Own Yorkshire Regiment

B1	J36
61076	65234
61396	

St Margarets Shed was the North British Railway's main depot in Edinburgh, with two 'A4's still, at this time, allocated to the shed and rostered for some of the Edinburgh Waverley to Aberdeen workings; whilst the employment of the class on the three-hour Glasgow–Aberdeen trains is a familiar tale to students of the end of the steam era.

My very brief visit to Edinburgh ended with departure the following morning from Waverley Station, on a photographically inglorious note with a blurred shot of 'B1' No. 61354, itself a St Margarets engine, coming off the 09.34 train from Hawick. I travelled in the cab of the 'Peak' diesel from Waverley to Liverpool, prior to a weekend's campaigning as prospective candidate for Birkenhead.

The following month I managed a visit to Goole on 4 September. Although having been on North Eastern territory, the shed was of Lancashire and Yorkshire heritage, and the motive power on view comprised Ivatt 'Flying Pigs' and WD 'Austerity' 2–8–0s, as ugly and unprepossessing motive power as is possible to imagine. Late that day, however, I 'scalped' four 'B1's at Wakefield: two in service and two dead on shed. For the record, their numbers were 61161/289/385/7.

If Goole had cocked a snook at its part-LNER heritage, then Derby, headquarters of the old Midland Railway, bastion of the LMS and mere outpost of the Great Northern, gained its revenge for LNER supporters. There, in the very heart of LMS country,

stood 'B1' No. 61237 *Geoffrey H. Kitson*, when I visited on 9 September 1966. Later that same day, on my way south, I stopped off at Banbury, once a busy inter-regional thoroughfare. Here, I made what transpired to be my last photo-call of an LNER locomotive, albeit dead inside the shed. 'B1' No. 61306, the engine concerned, was ultimately one of the last three survivors of a class that once numbered 409 members. At the time of my visit to Banbury, 61306 was allocated to Hull Dairycoates, being transferred to Low Moor in June 1967 for the last few weeks of her life. Withdrawn in September 1967 along with sisters 61030 and 61337, No. 61306 has survived into the preservation era, at the Main Line Steam Trust, Loughborough. *Railway Observer* (November 1967) reported that on 30 September, 61306 returned to Low Moor shed in the afternoon 'having returned from making two round trips with expresses between Bradford Exchange and Leeds City.' The same issue of *Railway Observer* reports, in the next column, the demolition of Leeds Central Station where, a few years earlier, I photographed an 'A1' Pacific (*see above*). That same issue of the magazine contained, under 'Withdrawals', the chilling entry 'B1' 61030 *Nyala* (56F), 61306/37[†] (56F)'.

That † marked the end: it was the sign of 'Class Extinct'. That, to all intents and purposes, was the end of active LNER steam on British Rail. From steam's birthplace in the industrial North-East, only the groaning, evil-smelling diesels remained behind: a sad end to a great tradition.

Previous page
Unsurprisingly, amongst my limited stock of LNER locomotives photographed in the twilight of steam, the 'B1' 4–6–0's predominate. Indeed by September 1966 there was precious little choice, yet Derby was not perhaps the most obvious place in which to find one. One of the named members of the class, No. 61237 *Geoffrey H. Kitson*, is turned on Derby Midland shed's turntable. The shed finally closed to steam in March 1967 and the buildings were demolished two years later. The Eastern heritage of this photograph stems not only from Thompson's 'B1' but from the fact that Derby was an outpost of the Great Northern Railway.

Methinks the fitters are needed here . . . but the shed looks pretty empty: not long left . . .

2 Between Turns

Overleaf
Canterbury is to the Church
of England, as Old Oak
Common shed was to British
steam – but sadly even this
great cathedral of steam
could not withstand the icy
blast of the diesel era.
Already rebuilding is well
under way on 23 January
1965, the last year of steam
working on the GWR main
line from Paddington. A
similar shot in an earlier book
brought a solitary query from
a correspondent, as to the
accuracy of my notes, which
on this occasion designate
these four pannier tanks as
57xx Class No. 9789: 94xx
Class No. 9404 and 8420: and
57xx Class No. 3608.
According to Volume One,
Part One of Peter Hands' new
series 'BR Steam Shed
Allocations' – another
treasure trove in the making
for enthusiasts – all four were
indeed allocated to 81A, Old
Oak Common, at the date of
this photograph. Note the
wooden-boarded turntable.
For me, the atmosphere as
much as the accuracy assists in
the renaissance of memory.

Railway enthusiasts were drawn to locomotive running sheds like bees to a honeypot, flies to flypaper – whatever the metaphor, there was an inevitable attraction. Possession of a permit, for unlimited visits, meant that one's constraint for a 'steam fix' was limited only by available time. Never having been addicted to drugs, I am unable to draw precise comparisons, but one felt instinctively the urge to 'get there' with one's camera.

As time goes by, the impossibility of recreating that intoxicating atmosphere of the big steam shed has finally, unwillingly become an accepted fact. Physically to recreate that atmosphere is beyond possibility. One has one's memories, there are the photographs, but Bctjcman notwithstanding, nor Kipling's '007', there are few if any words capable adequately of arousing the passionate – not a word to be used indiscriminately – the passionate emotions felt by the real enthusiast.

Often I am asked what it was about steam engines that so appealed to me. For over one hundred years, thousands upon countless thousands of our fellow-citizens have eulogised the steam railway. Be it the sight of a speeding train trailing white smoke through green valleys, over majestic viaducts, or emerging from graceful tunnels; or of a heavy freight, struggling up a gradient, pulling against the collar on damp, greasy rails; yet the shed surely remains the home and final resting place of the departed spirit of steam.

Did Betjeman ever visit Old Oak Common or St Philips Marsh roundhouses? I know not. His wholly delightful romanticism of the steam railway seems to have been related to its *public* appearances, at stations, in the country, or wherever it was 'on show'. I suppose that, in theatrical terms, the shed was 'backstage'. Perhaps that atmosphere of the star's dressing room, prior to the rise of the curtain, more truly excites, in its intimacy, the blood of *aficionados* of the theatre, than does the sight of the actors as the curtain rises for the public audience. Maybe that is

39

it: the engine shed was a private place, a secret world of railwaymen; and for the enthusiast, the chance to go 'backstage' was a chance to share the intimacy of the professional.

Sometimes it is said that there are vaguely indecent sexual overtones about the love of the steam-engine. Doubtless my colleague Julian Critchley could put it into words. Sometimes it is said that the machine itself personified for man his primeval mastery over the elements; mastery of fire, water, air. Indeed, the shed was a man's world, the vocabulary of which predated the invention of such phrases as 'sexual equality'. Shedmistress! Passed Firewoman! Thank heaven that our world of steam terminated before the advent of such trendy intellectualism as is today so beloved of (some) politicians, and 'social engineers'.

Perhaps then this chapter should have been entitled 'Curtain Up', were it not for the fact that the years of my railway photography, 1962–1968 were, all too often, a time when engine sheds were the scene of the last curtain call. The books and articles about the steam sheds still roll off the presses. That Peter Hands has truly earned my appreciation for his magnum opus 'What Happened to Steam' is not only a tribute to his research, diligence and attention to detail, but also a testimony to the astonishingly widespread interest in the *minutiae* of the facts of life of tens of thousands of individual steam locomotives.

They *were* individual. Each engine was a mistress to her driver and fireman, to be coaxed and cared for; even sometimes to be blasphemed at, kicked or cursed. If I need to apologise for thus romanticising, then so be it. Pass on, to the next chapter, perhaps the next book. For detailed history, accurate scientific explanation, mechanical appreciation, I am hopelessly inadequate. For shameless eulogy, uncritical emotion, unrequited love, stay here.

Keeping the show on the road was the main purpose of the running-shed. That is what it was – the *running* shed. This chapter, then, unlike 'This was Willesden', contains little research, but provides me unashamedly with a vehicle for showing shed scenes. As time elapses since the end of steam, it becomes tempting to regard shed scenes as merely an adjunct of the railway photographer's scenario. In reality, of course, the motive power depot was the heart of the railway operation. The railway was like a duck. Timetables were printed, tickets sold, meals prepared and served on buffet and restaurant cars, passengers waited at stations; this was the visible part of the duck, all smoothness, on the surface. Underneath, that duck had to paddle vigorously to make progress, and the steam-engine was the duck's furiously paddling feet. However smooth the duck's appearance on the surface, it was the motive power that provided the essential ingredient for movement.

Redhill Shed (75B), seemingly in the heart of 'electric country', remained an interesting place until its demise, in June 1965, of what had become the sole remaining Central Division steam shed. In addition to the freight workings, steam remained active on passenger workings on the SECR Reading–Guildford–Redhill–Tonbridge line, with Redhill acting as host to GWR 'Manors' as well as the Maunsell Moguls. The 'S15's were a familiar sight, and have always been one of my favourite classes, particularly the earlier Urie engines. Here, on 16 April 1963, Redhill's No. 30847 receives attention. One of the final Maunsell batch introduced in 1936, these locomotives were sturdy, powerful and reliable. With tractive effort of 29,855 lb they were slightly more powerful than the Urie engines, of a class of 45 in all. My shed pass was much prized, and visitors were not numerous, as may be deduced by the driver's expression of surprise. This engine is now preserved – at the Bluebell Railway, after more than 14 years languishing at Barry.

Note the lamp to the left of the vacuum brake, the water-column and semaphore signal – all reminders of an era gone.

The purpose of the shed, lest we forget, was to service, fuel, maintain, repair if necessary, the locomotives; but above all else, to get them to their trains on time, in good mechanical order. At a shed like Nine Elms, for example, in its latter days, split-second timing was essential when engines came off the shed, gained the main line between an often incessant stream of electric multiple units and backed down to Waterloo to head express trains to the South-West.

I am assuming that it is unnecessary, nor am I in any case qualified, to explain in detail, the technicalities of the motive power depot. Disposal of ash was just one of the problems associated with a steam shed, that reminds us of the unglamorous, indeed filthy, often dangerous work involved. To the men who worked there, it probably never seemed like a club, but the *esprit de corps* was an unspoken characteristic of the life of the true steam railway-man. To develop the analogy between club and shed would be to trivialise, maybe even to insult those men who kept the engines running. Yet just as a member enters his club and looks at the noticeboard, so the railwayman entered the shed and went straight to the blackboard on which the Engine Working Arrangements, or engine movements of the day, were listed. Roster details, amendments to the working timetable, permanent way work and speed restrictions, all had to be assimilated long before the driver and fireman took their steed off shed. Stores had to be visited, rag and lubricating oil acquired – the list of tasks to be undertaken, of knowledge to be acquired, of responsibilities to be accepted, was frankly beyond the comprehension of the average rail traveller then, and doubtless beyond an acceptable level of 'job specification' in today's world.

If the footplatemen were giants and heroes, at least they had the deserved and not inconsiderable satisfaction of public recognition, acclaim and endearment that is so noticeably absent today in the often sterile interface between footplatemen of neuter diesel or electric locomotives, let alone d.m.u's or e.m.u's, and the general public. For the fitters, cleaners and other shed staff, there was little glamour. Cleaning out great piles of soot and hot ash from the smokebox can hardly have rated as a pleasant task in itself. It was, of course, part of the job, a rung on the ladder which for some ended at the top link. Here then was the real difference that separated the steam railwayman from his modern counterpart, and which separated the railwayman from other workers. For there was a fierce loyalty to one's railway, and pride in the job, that pierced the dirt and the grime, the unsocial hours and the sheer physical effort. To make the point: in say 1909 or 1927, could there be any comparability between the feelings of the workforce on the LNWR or LMS, to the attitude of

Previous page
No chapter thus designated would be complete without a shot from London's last active main-line steam shed, Nine Elms. At its demise, some three years after this photograph was taken, it epitomised the death of British steam, and its atmosphere has been immortalised by that surpreme artist and good friend, David Shepherd. Here, on 7 July 1964, Eastleigh's Bulleid 'West Country' Pacific No. 34098 *Templecombe* is serviced and will now proceed to the turntable at the extremity of the shed to be turned. In the background a BR Standard has steam to spare.

Opposite
3 October 1964 was a magnificent day for colour photography, and even a mundane BR Standard '5' 4–6–0, such as No. 73170, seen here at Feltham, looked fine and dandy. The penultimate member of the class, she had a miserably short life-span from birth at Doncaster in May 1957 to withdrawal from Eastleigh shed in June 1966: a visible example of wasted investment on the sacrificial altar of 'modernisation'. 73170 spent most of her short life allocated to sheds in the North Eastern Region: Leeds (Holbeck), Scarborough and Royston, before coming south to Feltham and finally, at about the date of this photograph, to Eastleigh. Note the evil face of the future, in the background.

the coalminer of that era to his employer? Merely to pose the question is to answer it.

It has been said that, when nationalisation occurred, there were established five regions of British Railways, plus the GWR! Perhaps such a comment merely illustrates my personal proclivities, but can there ever have been a fiercer loyalty to 'the company' than that felt by the men of Swindon? Men, their pride, and 'their' engines; what a breed they were. Still today — perhaps even more today — the heroes of the footplate are household names to the railway enthusiast. Bill Hoole, Sam Gingell — names that have, for me, a grander ring than Fangio or Moss. And in what other industry was there ever a relationship, a knowledge, a respect (or occasionally a less attractive emotion) between the men who drove the machine and those who designed and built them? Was there a single solitary LNER man who knew not the name of Gresley? Or of LMS people, Stanier?

As usual I ramble on. With restraint, there may be room in this book for a chapter called 'Talking Steam'. Of my many proud and fond memories, perhaps the most notable was an afternoon spent in Calne, Wiltshire, in February 1981, with R. A. Riddles. Perhaps I abused my Parliamentary privilege by writing to him on House of Commons notepaper to ask him if I could call on him, meet him and record our conversation. He agreed, and his only proviso was that the contents of our conversation be not made public until after his death . . . Sitting and listening to him talking was literally to sit at the feet of the master, and to record history. It was not only what he said, about people with whom he was personally acquainted, from Bowen-Cooke to Bulleid; it was the actuality of conversing with someone, face to face, who really knew and had worked with these giants of steam.

The steam era did indeed breed giants. Not only the Chief Mechanical Engineers, or the Top Link drivers, but the Shedmasters too, were rarely dull nonentities. In the big sheds like Old Oak Common or St Philips Marsh, these men had charge not only of a very large workforce, and a large number of engines with all the concomitant responsibility; they were responsible for veritable cathedrals of steam in the great roundhouses. Not only the locomotives were mechanical either. Since the LNWR introduced the first mechanical coaling plant — at Crewe North Shed in 1910 — it is worth remembering the extent of mechanical equipment in a shed's machine shop and, often, numerous other areas. Then there was the turntable, and woe betide the foreman whose 'table' at a busy shed, broke down.

The range and extent of the steam shed's activity highlights the opportunities for photography, yet sadly few railway photographers bothered to record much beside the engines

As with Bulleid's 'Q1's, the 'USA' 0–6–0 tanks were unlikely ever to win a beauty contest, although they were functional and powerful. 14 of these locomotives, designed for the US Army Transportation Corps, were purchased by the SR in 1946. Declared redundant from Southampton Docks, the class was thereafter quite widely dispersed. No. 30072 is seen here at Guildford's unusual shed, the open-air turntable of which gave access to a covered roundhouse, on 2 January 1965. This was the final weekend of steam working on the cross-country Reading–Redhill line. Guildford shed provided the motive power for the Horsham line trains, handled at the end of steam mainly by Ivatt 2–6–2 tanks. 30072 has been preserved, and works on the Keighley and Worth Valley Railway. The cramped site of Guildford shed is now a car-park — yet again an ignominious fate for a once-living environment. See page 154 for an interesting comparison.

themselves. An exception is H. G. Forsythe, whose book *Steam Shed* is an excellent record of the life and atmosphere of its subject title. The working conditions left a lot to be desired, and a busy shed on a hot summer's day would send shudders through the Health & Safety Executive today. With thick smoke, very poor light, cramped conditions and limited space, indoor photography, let alone in colour, was a nightmare, particularly in straight sheds, as is apparent from my wretched efforts.

If one did not possess a permit, the challenge of obtaining entry far outweighed the thrill of the 'chase'; however, if one had a permit, then one could sometimes stray near or onto main lines, at locations where photographic permits would have been hard to obtain. Places like Nine Elms or Guildford, with third-rail electrification, come to mind. Even with my busy life, I managed to visit many steam sheds in their declining years. In the context of history, however, their demise was rapid indeed. In 1959, the year of Harold Macmillan's 'You've never had it so good' election victory, there were 470 steam sheds in active service on British Rail. The last three, Carnforth, Lostock Hall (Preston) and Rose Grove (Burnley) closed with the end of steam less than 10 years later.

In retrospect, steam's banishment was done with indecent

haste. Whereas the 1954 Modernisation Plan envisaged a gradual transition from steam to diesel and electric power, that plan was overtaken by the decision of the British Transport Commission (BTC) to eliminate steam as fast as possible, regardless of three factors that prudent businessmen would not have ignored. Firstly, many steam engines were still being built – *Evening Star*, the last, did not emerge from Swindon Works until 1960. Thus, an appalling waste of resources was authorised, in the name of 'modernisation' or 'image', rather than of prudence, planning or proper utilisation of scarce investment resources. Secondly, the diesels that were rushed into service as a result of an essentially 'political' decision by BR were untried, often unreliable and not infrequently unsuccessful. Thirdly, and writing with the benefit and wisdom of hindsight, the decision to replace coal-burning steam engines with oil-burning diesels, was taken in the days of cheap oil. Few then, in 1956, realised the portents of Suez on future oil prices.

So, steam was swept away. China, today, has a more enlightened railway motive power policy than had Britain 30 years ago. They are still building steam engines, but they use steam, diesel and electric, as appropriate. They cannot afford the luxury of allowing dogma to dictate their motive-power requirements. The

London Weekend Television's programme, 'South of Watford', has nothing to do with the town that has long been parodied as the place north of which civilisation ends. Watford shed itself seems rarely to feature in photographic albums, shaded into insignificance by the Willesdens and Camdens to the south, and the Rugbys and Crewes to the north; not to mention the numerous sheds serving the termini and junctions of the other lines northwards from London. However, 14 May 1964 was a splendid day, and BR Standard '2' 2–6–0 No. 78035 was disporting herself healthily 'at home' on Watford (1C) shed. Originally a sub-shed of Willesden, the duties of the engines allocated here included workings on the Rickmansworth and St Albans branches in the steam era. Less than a year after this photograph was taken, the shed had been closed, was soon demolished, and replaced by a new station car-park. Note the signal-box. 78035 was withdrawn in December 1965.

irony is that, even in the early 1960s, simple and inexpensive modifications to some of our steam engines, such as the fitting of the Kylchap double blast-pipe and chimney, to locomotives like the LNER 'A3's and 'A4's, and the GWR 'Kings' and 'Castles' significantly improved both the performance and care of these fine machines. The cost of these modifications was about £200 per engine . . .

Naturally, the BTC mandarins, non-railwaymen that many of them were, were damned if they wanted anyone to improve the efficiency and reduce the maintenance costs of the despised and hated steam-engine. 'Don't confuse me with the facts, I've made up my mind', is an attitude sometimes attributed to politicians, not to railwaymen: but then some of these people were not true railwaymen at all. It was, to quote Brian Haresnape, 'the mind of the accountant that condemned steam'.

So, steam was indeed condemned. The steam shed, for so long the heart of the steam railway, went too. Today, those boring, soulless diesels and electrics are housed in depots that, for the most part, reflect the characterless machines they house. One or two buildings from the steam age remain. For those wanting to try to recall the past, of the Big Four's main London motive power depots, the LNER's 'Top Shed' at Kings Cross has gone. On the LMS, Camden and Willesden have been flattened, too. On the SR, Nine Elms Shed was obliterated to make way for Covent Garden's new incarnation. Only the GWR's Old Oak Common has any structural remains left. But then it would be so: not even the maniacs of modernisation could quite destroy the GWR.

1985 is the GWR's 150th birthday. Steam has again climbed the South Devon banks, as 'Kings' and 'Castles' recreate the sight and sound of real trains, on Hemerdon and Dainton. Today's more enlightened BR management appreciates the history which still enthralls so many of our fellow-citizens. Just one small thought though: why did they insist that the 60 mph instruction, applied to all steam working now by BR, should not be broken on the Bristol-Plymouth run?

'Superbly maintained and enthusiastically driven loco-motives'? There were precious few of those about, as I recall, between 1962 and 1968. Yet it was lack of resources provided by management, not lack of interest by shed staff or footplatemen, that accounted for this sad state of affairs. In truth, much of the railway never really recovered from the damage and neglect of World War 2. Any successful business depends on a host of related factors: good relations, understanding and appreciation between managers and managed, loyalty, enthusiasm: in the heyday of steam, this was the rule, not the exception. Shed staff in those dying years kept the engines running in spite of senior

management disdain, disinterest in and disgust with steam. The buildings have now gone; the engines, the atmosphere, the spirit, too, are memories of yesteryear. Dirty, semi-derelict, dank, dripping, draughty places they were, at the end. Yet the sights, the sounds, perhaps above all the smell of the steam shed, can never be replaced, but will never, never be forgotten.

Bolton's first engine shed opened near the terminus of the Manchester–Bolton Railway in 1838. The 'new' shed, built in the 1870s and subsequently enlarged, remained intact to become one of the last Lancashire and Yorkshire Railway sheds to close, on 30 June 1968. Just five days previously I was there, to record some of the modern Stanier motive power denied by the LMS to this

3 Up the Grade

As already explained, the juxtaposition of text and photographs is my ambition: but it often proves easier to write, than to find the appropriate shots for such a chapter. This leads inevitably to scrutiny of the locations at which I took photographs. Exempting meteorological considerations there were three or four essential criteria governing my ability to select and visit suitable places. Firstly, one had to know where the gradients were. Secondly, they needed still to be steam-worked. Thirdly, I needed to have occasion to be reasonably adjacent thereto. Fourthly, one needed sufficient time available at the locations within the parameters of criteria one, two and three. It rarely happened.

Between the years 1962 and 1968, when my photo-mission was accomplished, I was trying to keep both my employer and my spouse, the long-suffering Jane, content: in other words, it was rarely possible to take days off work during the week, and not fair totally to neglect one's family responsibilities at weekends. Thus, visits to places which even the most ill-informed enthusiasts knew, like Shap or Beattock, fitted criteria one and two, but failed on three or four. There were few if any legitimate business reasons for me to spend hours in the wilds of Westmorland or Dumfriesshire (as they then were) and they were a very long way from home, in Berkshire.

Unfortunately, my knowledge of railway-photographic geography grew simultaneously albeit slowly with the decline in steam activity, thus compounding the problem. Any photography during the week was dependent on getting away from London with its office routine, yet naturally my time was spent in areas of commercial activity. This was fine for grabbing an hour here and there in Manchester or Liverpool, but the necessary knowledge of urban gradients was outwith my possession. I was dimly aware of Copy Pit by the end of steam, but the problem should be easily understandable.

This left weekends, and the need for proximity to home in

shed in earlier years. '8F' 2–8–0 No. 48775 and 'Black 5' 4–6–0 No. 45110 seem oblivious to the shed's imminent demise. 45110 was transferred, in those last hectic weeks, from Bolton to Carnforth and to Lostock Hall where she saw out the end of steam and today survives on the Severn Valley Railway as, by a curious coincidence, does 48773.

Berkshire. Obviously one preferred a destination guaranteeing steam, and now I could kick myself mightily. Jane and I regularly drove past Masbury Summit en route from Sunningdale to Burnham-on-Sea, home of her parents, yet the name never registered on my consciousness until it was too late. If only one could turn the clock back.

There were odd occasions when I was in the right place at the right time, but they were infrequent. I recall a snatched ten minutes at Patchway on 27 June 1964, which yielded a freight in charge of No. 6926 *Holkham Hall*, banked by '5101' Class 2–6–2T No. 4156. Perhaps the best place I visited was Manchester Victoria station, where trains faced the stiff climb up Miles Platting Bank. Eastbound parcel trains passing through the station on the middle lines often produced fireworks. (See page 117.) An attempt to capture the magnificent sight, let alone the sound, on an unforgettable day, 10 August 1967, turned out to have been almost worthless, due to camera malfocus caused by our labrador, Sam, who had had a session chewing my Voigtlander. The time I discovered the problem was when the film had been processed, and although I was in the Manchester area once or twice more that year, it was June 1968 before I returned to that particular location.

54

Above left and right
The poor quality of these two photographs are not attributable to the weather, but to my use of colour negative film from which transparencies have been processed twenty years later. My apologies.

On 26 June 1964, I parked the car beside the A38 at Patchway, and gained the embankment between up and down lines near this point. Ere long, making progress up the second of the lengthy series of gradients which leads ultimately from the Severn Tunnel to the southern plateau of the Cotswolds at Badminton, came a steam-hauled freight from South Wales. By this date, steam-hauled trains were a diminishing occurrence, so my heart sang at the sight of 4–6–0 No. 6926 *Holkham Hall* at the head of

the train (*above left*); and was
positively gleeful when the
banking engine hove into
view: '5101' Class 2–6–2T
No. 4156, of a class which
would soon be extinct, and of
which I had photographed
very few (*above right*).

Right
On 6 August 1965, business
took me from Glasgow to
Liverpool, and I managed to
talk myself into the cab of the
'Peak' diesel hauling the
train. My note recording the
driver's name has sadly
eluded me, so my thanks to
an unknown railwayman
who enabled me to take
almost my only photograph
on Shap. Climbing
northbound at Lambrigg, on
working 1S77, is 'Black 5'
4–6–0 No. 44759.

In the *Pre-Grouping Atlas & Gazeteer* (21/- net) is a list entitled 'Index to Summits'. There are 34, including the aforementioned Shap and Beattock. I did actually traverse both these famous gradients on 6 August 1965 in the cab of a 'Peak' diesel, and managed a few shots either through the windscreen or out of the window, of the steam-hauled trains that we passed. Of the remaining places listed, Lickey Incline is the only one to which I went for the sole purpose of railway photography. That was on 6 June 1964, and it rained, heavily and incessantly, all the time we were there. I say 'we' because my companion that day was Ed Chilton, at that time Managing Director of Rank Xerox. Never can one forget the sight of a 'Black 5' or 'Hall' or '9F' in charge of a freight on the 1 in 36 bank, with two or even three banking engines blasting away at the back. Indeed one such train was banked by a '9F' and two Pannier Tanks, and still made heavy weather of the wet rails. Photographing banking-engines at work is not an easy task at the best of times, but in gloomy light it is almost impossible to achieve worthwhile results.

As with so many other hobbies, railway photography attracts many people, but it is not an armchair activity. As steam succumbed, so those of us afflicted with the bug were forced to retreat into ever smaller enclaves, and most people seemed to

The Lickey Incline: Mecca for anyone seeking to witness the cruel struggle up a notorious main-line gradient. By 6 June 1964, GWR steam here was already rare. It was an absolutely foul day of incessant heavy rain, which would have dampened the ardour and enthusiasm of all save those with a mission to experience a sight and sound that would very soon be gone forever. Banking up from Bromsgrove was in the hands of '9F' 2–10–0's and Pannier tanks, that afternoon. The only GWR locomotive to put in an appearance at the head of a train was No. 5984 *Linden Hall*, seen here in dreadful light for colour photography, making slow but steady progress up the 1 in 36. She was banked by '94xx' Pannier No. 9493, and '9F' No. 92230. I can remember that afternoon as though 'twere yesterday.

gather at the obvious locations. In the high, open places like Shap, congestion was probably never a problem until the very end of steam. Solitude, however, is an essential ingredient of my railway photography; where the full force of the elements in the high fells was matched by the brave struggle of defiant steam power, there must have been a fellow feeling between man, his created beast and the landscape. Never did I manage so to arrange my affairs as to be able to experience this terrain. It is my loss, which I mourn and I cannot pretend that the same atmosphere pervaded the struggle of a 'Jinty' to move a rake of empty stock on wet rails at Edge Hill carriage sidings. Nevertheless, artistically I believe that the challenge of urban photography outweighed the difficulties faced against the backdrop of Loups Fell or the Lune Gorge. For the railway photographer, to create space is more difficult than to use it when readily available.

How dull it all is, now. Groaning diesels convey none of the struggle against the grade that epitomised the days of steam. As for the electrics, they make the very title of this chapter redundant. Better it is to contemplate the struggles of building the lines, with their sweeping curves and magnificent viaducts, than to seek to extract any worthwhile emotion from modern motive power.

Lest it be thought that gradients were put into railway lines purely for the benefit of railway photographers, it has to be said that the great engineers did their best to avoid them. Severe operating difficulties were a concomitant of steep gradients, precise details of which had to be known, appreciated, felt by the enginemen. Amongst my book collection is a London & South Western Railway Gradient Manual, dated 1887. It reached me as a pile of mouldering papers buried under generations of bumf in the foreman's office of one of the last LSWR sheds to be demolished. Printed by Waterlow & Sons it belonged to 'Mr Stone, N. Elms, June 1887'. Many of the lines have long since gone, such as two that ran through part of my constituency, the 'Salisbury and Dorset Line' and the 'Ringwood and Christchurch Branch'. The 'Somerset and Dorset Railway', 'North Cornwall Line', 'Holsworthy Branch' — are but reminders of the past.

With the advent of the TGV in France, railways built in the era of electric traction are merely cross-country motorways laid with rails. Indeed the TGV engineers, unlike the motorway builders, do not even bother to skirt the hills or to seek the flattest route. The straight line, as Brian Haresnape pointed out when 'correcting' my original manuscript, is the order of the day. For the contemporary railway engineer, gradients have become operationally irrelevant.

4

This was Willesden

This example of Alan Godfrey's reproductions of historic Ordnance Survey maps of areas of specific railway interest illustrates the railway lines at Willesden Junction, identifying their heritage and nomenclature. By the date of this map – 1915 – the railway formation was virtually complete, and with minor changes remains intact today. The area illustrated covers three contemporary Ordnance Survey sheets, so Alan Godfrey does an immense service to students of railway history. In thanking him, I thoroughly recommend his series to anyone wishing to study specific locations.

The Engine Shed to the south of the Grand Junction Canal is Old Oak Common, whilst Willesden Shed (1A) is at the top left of the map. The Carriage Sheds to the right of Willesden Junction Station is now the site of the electric Motive Traction Depot (MTD).

There are many places which owe their fame to the railway; towns like Crewe or Swindon are obvious examples. Other locations exist or existed only as railway destinations – places like Riccarton Junction or Trent, for example. Yet again, villages like Box with its tunnel, or Shap with its incline, are renowned for their railway connection. Usually, but not always, these places are distant from the largest cities of the land and often remote. In London, however, are places totally enclosed within urban growth, yet identified by railway nomenclature. The Number 19 bus goes to Clapham Junction, which has for generations been an identifiable area in its own right. Doubtless thousands who now live there have never been on to the station platforms, or even know that it exists. Dalston Junction is another, perhaps less renowned. But Willesden Junction surely claims supremacy above all others in the capital, for it was the site not only of two important suburban stations, large carriage sheds, gas works, wagon repair shop and extensive freight yards; it was 1A – Willesden Motive Power Depot.

It is true that Camden Shed housed the glamorous passenger engines of the London & Birmingham, later the London & North Western Railway, and this is not an attempt to gainsay Camden's role. But Willesden Junction was a 'railway town' within the capital, albeit beyond the inner urban confines when first it was developed. The complex merited a lengthy article in the *Railway Magazine* of 1897. Yet, unlike true 'railway towns', Willesden, and indeed Willesden Junction, has always seemed a place apart. Whereas in your Crewes and Swindons, Darlingtons and Eastleighs, the railways were part of the broader community, in Willesden the railway seemed to be a separate, but totally pervasive entity, almost as though the area was all railway and nothing else.

My first conscious arrival there was at the first stop out of Euston for the Uppingham School special train in 1948: not that such an awesome journey, for a new boy, featured railway

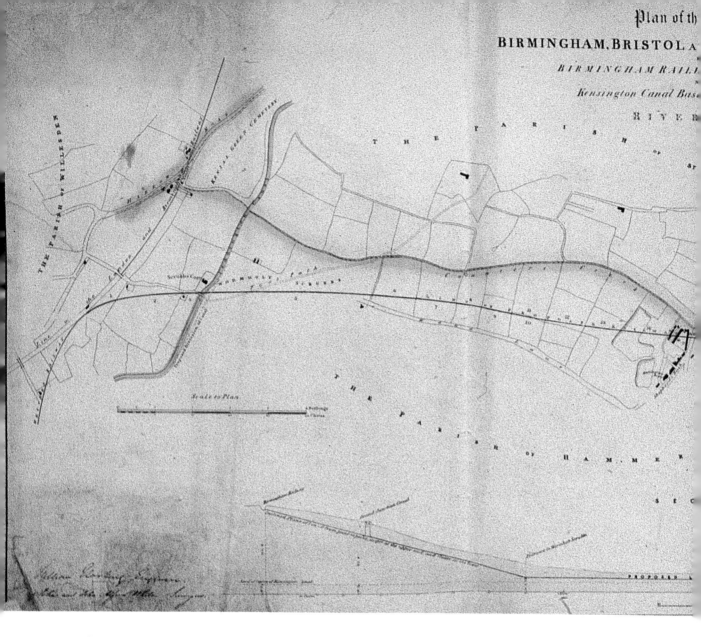

interest as a priority. Even then it seemed a strange place; one wondered why the train stopped there, as over the years on 'School Specials' no boys seemed ever to get on or off. Indeed, as a passenger station, Willesden Junction never approached in importance the role of Willesden as locomotive depot, parcels or goods station.

By the time that I first visited the shed, with camera, in February 1963, Camden's steam allocation had formally been transferred there; but my interest in Willesden has led me into some fascinating research for this chapter.

In previous books, my use of Ordnance Survey maps and British Rail archive material has enabled me to highlight aspects of social change wrought by the railway on the landscape, as well

Dated as early as 1836, this 'Plan of the Proposed Line of the Birmingham, Bristol and Thames Junction Railway' reminds us, by its title, of the dawn of the railway era, when travel by rail from Birmingham to Bristol was via Euston and Paddington and, even after the construction of this line, was still via London. The fascination of old maps is heightened by the spelling, such as 'Wormholt Scrubbs'

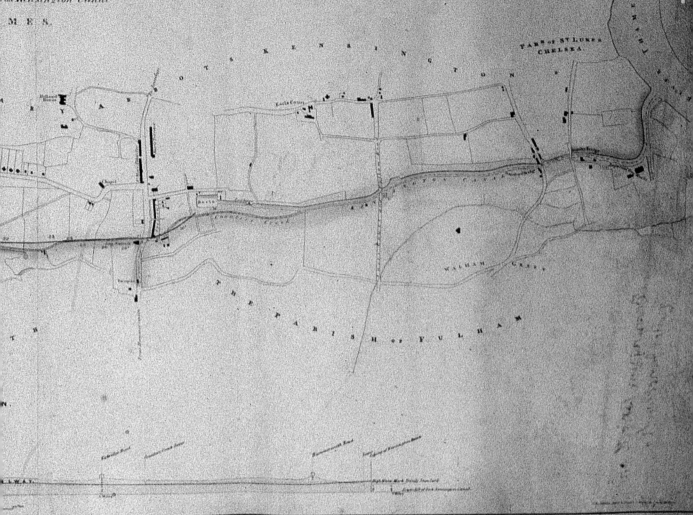

and 'Holsden Green'. Many of the villages and hamlets around Willesden seem considerably to have changed their names in the last 150 years. The Birmingham, Bristol and Thames Junction soon was retitled the West London. (Dare I mention that this map predates the Great Western's main line – the reference at the extreme left to 'Western Railway' being the N&SW Junction line.)

as demonstrating in detail certain aspects of railway history and railway development itself. Pondering how this pattern might be extended into a new area, an obvious source of material presented itself; it has the additional attraction of being readily available and accessible to me without leaving the building where I spend much of my life – the Palace of Westminster. At the far end of the first floor corridor in the House of Lords is a remarkable man, in charge of an even more remarkable archive, Harry Cobb, Clerk of the Records in the House of Lords Records Office. Perhaps the nature and potential of these records, to railway enthusiasts, can be appreciated by recognising two points and merging them. Firstly, all new public railway construction since time immemorial has required Parliamentary approval, which itself

61

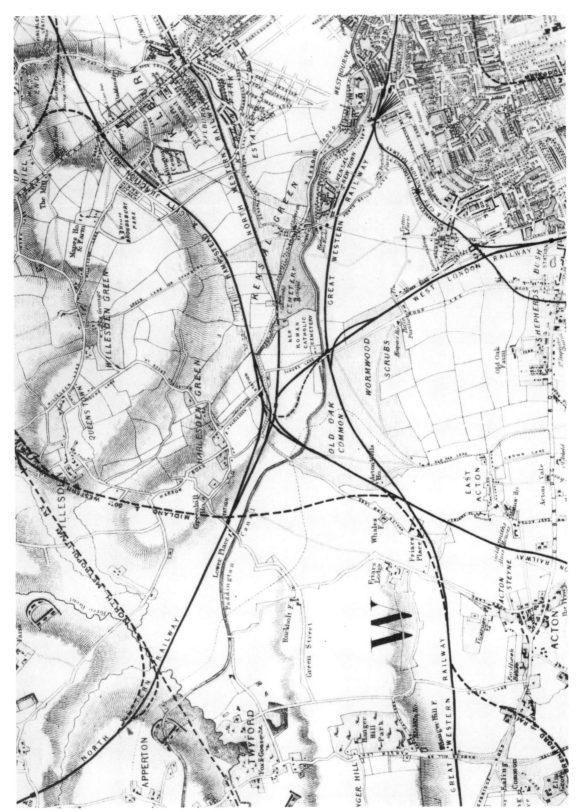

Dated 1867, this map is extracted from the archives in the House of Lords to which extensive reference is made on adjacent pages. My difficulty has been one of elimination. This in fact is a small section of a map entitled 'A NEW MAP OF METROPOLITAN RAILWAYS AND MISCELLANEOUS IMPROVEMENTS' and is included within the deposited papers in connection with the Midland and South Western Junction Railway – the one via Willesden that is, not via Swindon!

As ever there is much of topographical interest in what was still mainly a rural landscape. Londoners will notice how the spelling of places has evolved: between 1836 as seen on the map on pages 60–1, and 1867 as seen here, 'Holsden' has become 'Harlesden', but 'Apperton' has not yet become 'Alperton'. The fact that these early lines were not 'suburban' or 'commuter' routes – words not yet invented – but were inter-railway links accounts for their survival, almost intact, to this day.

Perusal of and comment on these maps tempts me to stray beyond the bounds legitimately encompassing an author of a railway book; so perhaps a study of the evolution of Willesden's railway lines and stations is the more appropriate detail to which I should direct your attention, as between this map and that on page 76.

inevitably necessitates full and minute details of land ownership and occupation to be examined, debated and approved, amended or rejected by Parliament. Secondly, the importance of the archives is best summarised in Mr Cobb's own words, delivered in a lecture at the Conference of the Economic History Society in 1964:

The importance of the documents in the custody of the House of Lords for the study of political and constitutional history has been recognised by historians from the time of Lord Macaulay onwards. The value of these records for economic history has, however, been appreciated only in more recent years and even this appreciation has been confined to a small number of subjects in the field. Some historians doubtless still imagine, from the name of the repository, that its contents relate mainly to political matters or to the history of the peerage. The fact is, however, that the documents there dealing with economic and social matters far exceed in quantity those which are of a political or biographical nature.

The records which are now in the care of the Lords Records Office consist chiefly of: the archives of the House of Lords from 1497 onwards; a few, post-medieval, House of Commons documents which survived the fire of 1834; and a large proportion of the Commons records which have accumulated since that time. The sources for economic history which are to be found amongst these records fall into three main groups: first, those which relate to the public business of both Houses and in particular to proceedings on public Bills; secondly, the private Bill records of both Houses, which are by far the largest group; and lastly, a very varied accumulation of 'Papers laid on the Table of the House of Lords'.

This is not a history book, and I have no pretensions in that direction, but it is perhaps worth quoting two more paragraphs from Mr Cobb's lecture, which itself has been reprinted by the House of Lords Record Office:

Other (miscellaneous) documents relating to Private bills were deposited in the House of Lords, particularly during the first half of the nineteenth century. Thus, a number of turnpike toll accounts are to be found amongst the papers and these were produced (presumably) to support the declarations made, with many turnpike Bills, that the capital required for new work could be borrowed on the security of the tolls collected on existing roads. Again, estimates of the traffic expected on a new road or railway might be deposited, such as those for the

Oxford and Great Western Union Railway Scheme of 1837. Some indication of the range of questions which were put to witnesses is to be found in a Commons Standing Order of 1836 which laid down that committees on railway bills were to inquire into, and report on, each bill in respect of twenty separate considerations. These included: the amount of capital to be employed in the scheme and the identity of the subscribers to it; 'The sufficiency or insuffiency for agricultural, commercial, manufacturing or other purposes of the present means of transport and communication between the proposed termini, stating the present amount of traffic by land and water, the average charges made for passengers and goods, and the time occupied'; the number of passengers, and weight and description of goods, expected on the proposed railway; the income expected from the railway; whether competing lines existed and if so was the proposed line superior or inferior to them; the engineering difficulties which might be encountered and 'any other circumstances of which the House should be informed'.

My appetite thus whetted, my choice for location fell on Willesden Junction, for reasons explained earlier in this chapter.

The first station at Willesden opened in 1841 and is referred to on page 65. For making this historic photograph available, I am indebted to the Brent Library Service and to Valerie Bott at the Grange Museum in Neasden Lane, wherein lies a wealth of early Willesden material. When the London and Birmingham Railway first opened, this station was not envisaged, as, according to *Railroadiana: a new History of England 1838*, Harrow was 'the first station on the London and Birmingham Railroad'.

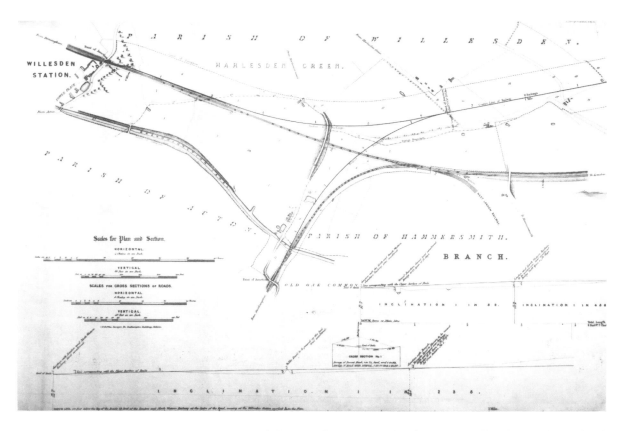

Plan and section detail from the deposited papers in Parliamentary Session 1852–3, for the North and South Western, Hampstead and City Junction Railway. This is a vital piece of the Willesden jigsaw, and cross-reference with the Railway Clearing House map on page 76 will illustrate this. Again, only the rural nature of the terrain made the construction of so many lines a feasible proposition.

Now part of the London Borough of Brent, Willesden is described in the *London Encyclopaedia* thus: 'Until the 19th century it was a rural area of exceptional charm with small hamlets such as Neasden and Harlesden, a few large houses, farms and the village of Willesden itself.'

As with so much of the countryside around London, it was the coming of the railway that transformed country villages and fields into spreading suburbia. The population appears to have been static at 750 between 1811 and 1851. With the opening of the London & Birmingham Railway came the first railway structure, a wayside station opened in 1841 to serve the local communities, and sited three-quarters of a mile on the country side of that railway's junction with the West London Railway. The early history of this first station, situated on Acton Lane, is sparse. Originally there were two up and two down trains calling daily, and indeed contemporary anecdote had it that one Captain Mark Huish, latterly General Manager of the London & North Western Railway (LNWR) who lived nearby at Harlesden House, was the beneficiary for whom the station was built (This seems disproven.) It was a long way from Willesden village. In 1844 an interchange station opened, and closed. The London & Birmingham in due course (16 July 1846) was absorbed within the

London & North Western Railway; and the LNWR features large in the subsequent railway growth hereabouts. In 1853 another junction was formed, when there opened a new line, linking with the LNWR and the North and South Western Junction Railway which itself joined the LNWR to the London and South Western Railway at Kew. This new line had been duly authorised by Parliament in the 1853 session, and was known at its inception as the North and South Western Hampstead and City Junction Railway this line 'being intended to commence by a junction with the Main Line of the London and North Western Railway, in the parish of Willesden, in the county of Middlesex, at or near the Willesden Station on that Main Line, and terminating by a junction with the East and West India Docks and Birmingham Junction Railway, in the parish of Saint Pancras, in the said county, at or near the point where such last mentioned Railway crossed the road leading from Camden Town to Highgate, and which road is called the Kentish Town Road, and such Branch Railway being intended to commence by a junction with the said intended Railway in the said parish of Willesden, at or near a mile-post on the south side of the road leading from London to Harrow, called the Harrow Road, indicating four miles to London, and to terminate by a junction with the North and South Western Junction Railway, in the parish of Acton in the said county, at a point on that Railway one hundred and twenty yards or thereabouts southward of the bridge carrying such Railway over the Grand Junction Canal.'

The almost incomprehensible complexities of railway development in Willesden were mirrored elsewhere, in London and some of our major cities, but at Willesden the network evolved over a considerable period. In 1860 the completion of the Hampstead Junction line saw Willesden as the point of convergence of three tributary lines, but its only station was still what was described in Edwin Course's *London Railways* as 'the modest establishment on the country side of the Junction'. In the hope that confusion may turn to clarity – both for passenger and reader! – let me quote again from Course:

This state of affairs ended in 1866 when Willesden Junction was opened – three years after Clapham. To provide access from all directions, two new link lines were constructed. First, the junction with the Hampstead line was east of the old station but west of the new one, so that all trains from the Hampstead direction running out towards Harrow would miss the new station. This was overcome by a spur leaving the HJR to join the main line *east* of Willesden. Second, it was desired to give a through run from the HJR to the WL and this was achieved by

Endless sheets of handwritten documents are appended to innumerable railway Bills. There is nothing particularly significant about this one, but it is included in order to illustrate the extent of the detailed effort implicit in seeking Parliamentary approval to build a new railway. To browse amongst all these old documents is to appreciate, even to share in, the sense of excitement bred of the ingenuity, enthusiasm, imagination, determination and ambition of our forebears for the rights to railway development.

In Parliament.

Session 1853.

North and South Western (Hampstead and City Junction) Railway Bill.

Statement in pursuance of Standing Order No. 182, Section 10.

The total length of the space which is intended or sought to be taken for the proposed Works and to give up which the consent of the Owners of the Land has not been obtained is five miles, four furlongs and eighty links and the greatest breadth of land required to be taken in each inclosure belonging to each such Owner together with the names of such Owners and the heights above the surface of all proposed Works on the ground of each such Owner are stated in Appendix A.

The names of the Owners or Rate-paying Occupiers of Houses situate within 300 yards of the proposed works who have before the 31st December prior to the introduction of the Bill into Parliament sent to the Promoters of the Railway their dissent from or any written objections to the Railway are set forth on Appendix B.

a spur passing over the main line and curving round to join the WL at Mitre Bridge Junction. The new station consisted of three rather confusing parts – the main line platforms, high level platforms on the spur from the HJ to the N and SWJ, and more high-level platforms on the spur from the HJ to the WL. The two high-level stations were at opposite ends of the main line platforms, and as up North London trains left alternately from the N and SWJ and the WL ends, there were sad stories of intending passengers running perpetually along the main line platforms from one high level to the other but always just missing the trains. Relief came in 1885 when, by linking the south end of the WL station to the N & SWJ, all trains could use that station. The old spur between the HJ and the N & SWJ was abolished in 1892 – its only surviving relics are some earthworks and the remnants of a bridge abutment by the side of the main line. Then in 1894 major rebuilding operations were undertaken, including new premises to cope with the greatly increased traffic at the one high-level station which now carried the traffic of the two. In 1912 the New Station, consisting of a large island platform with a double track bay at the London end, was opened with steam services. It was on the north side of the station and the spur from the HJ was diverted from the existing main line to run into the new line. (The curve of the abandoned alignment is reflected in the curve of the wall of one of the sheds.) Willesden Junction received a major facelift in 1955, but the station, with its 15 platforms, has not changed *fundamentally* since 1912.

That was a clarification! Since then, Willesden Junction Main Line Station has been totally demolished, as part of the West Coast Main Line (WCML) electrification: but let me return briefly to the earlier years and the time prior to the moment when, as Course says, 'Relief came in 1885 . . .'.

The high-level platform served the two points at which the Hampstead Junction made its connections. Each point had its own station. Trains departed at half-hourly intervals for the City, but passengers were given no indication from which of the stations the next train would depart. The low-level platforms served the main line. With a labyrinth of entrances and passages, the complex was known locally as 'Bewildering Junction' or 'The Wilderness'. If you wish to study all this, the map on page 58 should help.

Having mentioned the role of Parliament in the construction of new lines, and having sought to illustrate the point with extracts from Parliamentary papers and charts, it is necessary for the

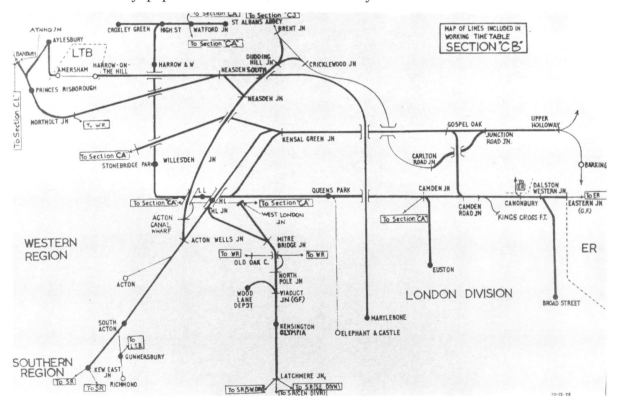

purpose of this chapter to remind ourselves that its importance was always related to its railway significance, as depot and junction, rather than to its usefulness to people. By 'people', of course, I refer to railway travellers rather than to the very large number of people who were employed by the various railway installations that served the area.

This is not to denigrate either the importance or usefulness and traffic-level of Willesden Junction station in its heyday; rather is it to emphasise the importance of the railway activity not immediately related to the direct service of the traveller. Indeed, Willesden Junction today remains a convenient centre for anyone wanting to travel around London: but one wonders who actually realises this? Although since WCML electrification there is no longer a station on the LNWR-cum-LMS-cum-BR main line route from Euston (why *did* the Uppingham School service stop there?), there is a frequent service from the 'New' station direct to Euston; to Broad Street there were two routes; via Gospel Oak to Barking; via Camden Road to Stratford and North Woolwich; to Watford (with direct connections to the North); and via the old North and South Western Junction Railway to Kew and Richmond. The Broad Street services were terminated during 1985 with the closure of this historic station and its immediate conversion to a pile of rubble.

It was in fact very much an LMS place when first I visited Willesden with my camera; although much of the railway superstructure was of LNWR vintage, including those delightful lower-quadrant signal gantries that, together with the 'Jinties' and the 'Black 5's, the '8F's and 'Coronations' seems hard to reconcile with today's West Coast Main Line. However, in spite of electrification, modernisation and resignalling on the main line, the railway architecture and paraphernalia on the other lines – the erstwhile North London, North and South Western Junction, the North and South Western Hampstead and City Junction, even the New lines – contain ample and self-evident reminders of yesteryear. Of the area of Willesden MPD however the obliteration is total. I have recently photographed the area where once the shed stood. It is so painful and so barren that it does not merit inclusion.

Willesden MPD, being the LNWR and then the LMS main locomotive repair shop and freight engine-shed in London, was usually dominated by freight and shunting locomotives, until almost the end of its life, which came on 27 September 1965. In the preceding two years, following the closure to steam of Camden Shed on 9 September 1963 (its steam allocation had already been ended), Willesden was allocated more of the glamorous 'named' locomotives than in at least the previous

From detailed hand-drawn plans to printed extracts from today's BR Working Timetable is a quantum jump. The stylised chartography shown here is reproduced from the London Midland Region Working Timetable for Section 'CB', covering the area identified as 'London, Richmond, Watford and Branches (excluding Main Line)'. Its validity was the period 14 May 1984 to 12 May 1985.

For those unfamiliar with working timetables, the map is of course stylised, similar to that of the London Underground. The services within the timetable relate to the routes shown with the thick black line: thus the main (LNWR) line services from Euston to the North are not included within section 'CB', but are in a separate timetable, section 'CA', to which reference can be seen.

The pivotal importance of Willesden is well illustrated here, for on this one map can be seen reference also to the territory of Southern, Western and Eastern Regions. This map will need to change with the closure of the line to Broad Street.

All movements – passenger, parcel, freight, empty stock, light engine, special – are timetabled, but naturally amendments and supplements are frequently issued. My thanks to British Rail for permission to use this material.

century of its existence. Still, vis-à-vis Camden, it was over the years the main depot for heavy service repairs of passenger locomotives from Camden, which sent its Pacifics and 4–6–0s there as required. Indeed, three of the last four engines to leave Camden for Willesden were 'Coronation' class Pacifics, one of which, No. 46240 *City of Coventry*, I photographed at Willesden on 5 July 1964. During those two years from September 63–65, Willesden's halycon days, an Indian summer of express passenger engines, I saw and photographed 'Coronations', 'Scots', a rebuilt 'Patriot', 'Jubilee's and 'Britannia's, the latter for servicing when in use on surviving Great Central semi-fasts; but all usually in cramped and photographically-awkward situations. The condition of these locomotives was often deplorable.

Notwithstanding the former Camden passenger locomotives, however – Camden was a running shed – Willesden remained until the end mainly a freight shed, where eight-coupled engines were the staple diet, and 'Jinties' were always in evidence. 'Black Fives' naturally were there aplenty, as well as '4F's, '8F's and 2–6–4 tanks of Fowler, Stanier and Fairburn design. Towards the end, BR Standard 78xxx Moguls appeared, helping out with the freight, ballast, empty stock and shunting turns, until finally, electrification of the West Coast Main Line brought about the

Above left
'Of the motive power comparisons, there could be few greater contrasts, accentuated by the paraphernalia of the overhead electric-traction equipment.' Even in 1963, the sight of a 'Black 5' standing at the head of a stationary train was barely enough to raise the camera to the eye, whilst the ephemera of LNWR signals attracted little detailed inquisitiveness or specific photography from the average railway enthusiast with camera. No. 45329 stands beneath Old Oak Lane Bridge on 23 February that year. There was almost incessant marshalling, shunting and shed-related activity on and around the main line. Today, the steam shed has gone and, whilst the occasional diesel shunter potters about, the

main activity comprises a regular procession of fast-moving electric trains, raising the dust on the site where once stood Willesden Junction Main Line Station.

Above right
'With Ivor at my side, understandably fretting as I photographed electric locomotive-hauled expresses whistling past my ear at 100 mph, . . .'

The ugliness of the overhead electric equipment matches the anonymity of the electric locomotives, let alone the e.m.u.'s. It is the history of Willesden, and the geography related to that history, rather than 'the trains', that today retain the fascination of this place.

eclipse of steam. I never saw Willesden with those splendid LNWR 0–8–0s: engines that I loved even though I never saw one.

My personal knowledge of Willesden was restricted to its last few years. Brian Haresnape, however, in 'vetting' this chapter, recalls his first visit to Willesden, in 1944, when he saw a 'locomotive with ''USA'' on its tender – very impressive to my young eyes (a 2–8–0 of course) and in the 1945–47 period there was a complete wartime Ambulance Train parked in a siding just to the north-east of the High Level Station'. He recalls an 'incredible variety' of locomotives from all four companies working over the West London line, many of them having a difficult job climbing the gradient from North Pole Junction up to and over the bridge carrying the line over the GWR main line at Old Oak. The top of that gradient was the extremity of my 'return to Willesden' in the gathering of material for this chapter. Brian also suggested a mention of Devons Road Shed, Bow, which, apart from a small sub-shed at Acton, closed in 1916, was the North London Railway's (NLR) only depot, at which was based that company's entire locomotive fleet. The NLR was absorbed by the LNWR from 1 February 1909, from which date the latter company ensured, by the nature of railway geography, that Devons Road and Willesden were actively intertwined, and the

Appropriately allocated to Carlisle (Upperby) for many years, 'Coronation' 4–6–2 No. 46238 *City of Carlisle* was a visitor to Willesden on 5 July 1964. It is galling to think that, just four months later, she was to be withdrawn, and before the year was out, scrapped at West of Scotland Shipbreaking, Troon.

Willesden shed had just over a year to go before closure at this date, on which I was fortunate enough to photograph two more of Stanier's Pacific masterpieces, No. 46240 *City of Coventry* and 46241 *City of Edinburgh*. The former was actually allocated to Willesden, having been transferred 'down the road' on the closure of Camden MPD, whilst the latter was an Edge Hill engine until withdrawal just two months after I saw her at Willesden that day.

As with most sheds, Willesden was a forest of posts and poles, all there to thwart railway photographers.

shed was in fact coded 1D when it was transferred to the London Midland Region's Western Division in 1949. Brian recalls Devons Road engines – 'Jinties' and Ivatt Moguls – constantly working at Willesden High Level. Sadly, this was before my arrival on the scene.

With their usual courtesy and helpfulness, British Rail facilitated that 'return to Willesden' on 5 November 1984.

After three or four exceptionally fine, bright November days, it was with hope and anticipation that I awoke that morning of 5 November: but this had nothing whatsoever to do with a Parliamentarian's recollections of Guy Fawkes! The thought of returning to Willesden Junction for the first time for nearly 20 years was frankly exciting, even in the era of bland diesel and electric motive power. I was 10 minutes early for my appointment with Stephen Ollier, Area Mechanical and Electrical Engineer, London Area, West Coast Main Line.

Much has happened, not just to the railways but to me, since the end of steam. For a start I have become known as a consistent champion of British Rail at Westminster. Furthermore, these words you are reading are in my fifth railway book to be published since 1979. Thus my requests to BR for facilities to visit are generously granted; and my reception on arrival at my destination is invariably welcoming. This day was no exception.

Railway enthusiasm is a totally classless occupation, and one needs to make neither apology nor explanation of one's interest, to professional railwaymen. In response to his invitation to me to state my ambitions and requirements, I explained to Stephen Ollier my twin purposes: to revisit the sites of the locations at and from which I had taken photographs, in the years 1963–65; and to examine in detail, on the ground, the railway geography and industrial archaeology of Willesden Junction. In a trice he ascertained my needs, and asked Ivor LeFevre to join us in his office. Whereas Stephen Ollier was a comparative newcomer to the vicinity, Ivor had spent his life there. With 13 relatives at one time or another working for the railway, from LNWR through LMS to BR, and including both his son and daughter amongst the current list, he was clearly the perfect guide.

'Did you know 1A?' I asked.

'And 1B and 1C as well', he replied.

At a stroke I had acquired the guidance of a man steeped in personal working knowledge of Willesden, Camden and Watford steam sheds. He had started as an apprentice, rising through the grades of fitter to Maintenance Foreman.

'Is there a shed here still?'

'Yes, the traction maintenance depot is over there', he said, pointing towards the Euston side of the building.

Ugh! So TMD has to replace MPD as the modern London Midland Region nomenclature. For me, that was the least interesting part of my visit to Willesden Junction. Who on earth wants to bother to look at lifeless electric and diesel engines in a boring modern building? In fact, the TMD has been built on the site of the former south carriage shed. The old north carriage shed, and both the steam running sheds – roundhouse and 12 road straight – have gone.

In the knowledgeable and agreeable company of Ivor LeFevre I spent over five hours tramping the bounds of Willesden Junction. It is, of course, an 'area', not just a junction. To relate minute by minute my impressions, reminiscences and thoughts would be tedious in the extreme. Yet for anyone interested in railway history, such a visit is thoroughly worthwhile. I hope that the maps and plans included in this chapter, as well as the odd photograph, may whet your appetite, although do not attempt a visit without permission.

In response to Ivor's request, we began by retracing my steps to the site of my first photo-visit to Willesden Junction, on 23 February 1963, which began on the platforms of the 'old' West Coast Main Line station, which had seven through platforms and two bays. A victim of the Beeching 'rationalisation', that old station no longer exists. Just prior to its closure and subsequent demolition it had less than 30 trains calling daily; most passenger traffic used the 'New' station – built in 1894 – which had and still has the electric train service, both BR to Euston and until recently Broad Street, and the LT Bakerloo Line service, now re-commenced again north of Queen's Park.

For anyone seeking a 'then and now' comparison, there could be few more dramatic changes than to stand at the north end of what was Willesden Junction Main Line station, under the bridge that carries Old Oak Lane over the railway. I recalled trespassing off the end of the platform and under the bridge, where I would hide to take photographs. My very first shot, that gloomy winter's afternoon, shows a Willesden long gone. In asking you to excuse the quality of the photographs, at least their use enables me to share with you the pangs of melancholia which swept over me as I retraced my steps. Through the second arch of the bridge, 1A 'Jinty' No. 47501 was pottering along; through the next arch, an unidentified 'Black Five' was blowing off at the head of a freight; visible through the arch on the right is one of the many manual signal boxes in the vicinity. (Happily five, albeit not this one, still survive, but not for too much longer it seems.)

To endeavour to juxtapose any photograph of Willesden '84 with Willesden '63 hereabouts is not easy. The road over-bridge is one constant feature. In the distance of my third shot that day,

1A. Lacking perhaps the style and glamour of Old Oak Common just down the road, Willesden Shed was essentially a workaday place, but it had an aura of importance commensurate with its size and strategic location. Of it, there remains no trace whatsoever. To return in search of memories is a barren experience. 23 February 1963 was the date of my first visit. This was Willesden . . .

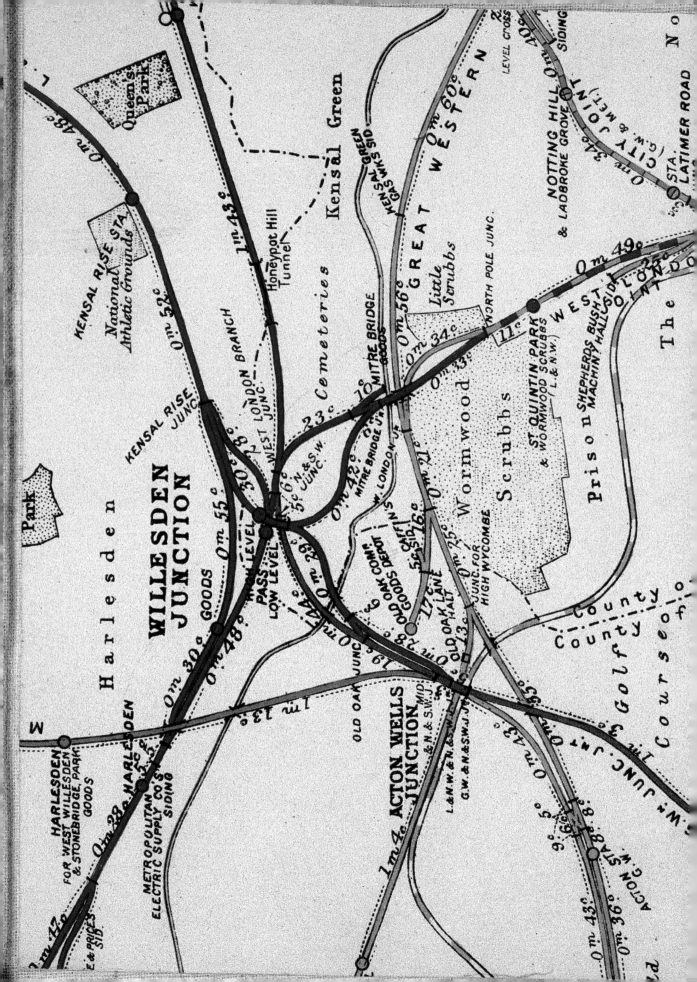

QUEEN'S PARK

0m 48c

Kensal Green

GREAT WESTERN

0m 60c

LEVEL CROSS

0m 40c

CITY JOINT (G.W. & Met.)

STA. LATIMER ROAD

0m 34c

NOTTING HILL & LADBROKE GROVE

SIDING

No.

National Athletic Grounds

KENSAL RISE STA.

0m 52c

KENSAL GREEN

KENSAL WKS SID.

Little Scrubbs

NORTH POLE JUNC.

0m 56c

0m 49c

0m 25c

WEST LONDON

The

1 in 43c

Honeypot Hill Tunnel

Cemeteries

MITRE BRIDGE GOODS

0m 34c

0m 33c

11c

ST. QUINTIN PARK & WORMWOOD SCRUBBS (L. & N.W.)

SHEPHERDS BUSH MACHIN'Y HALL SID.

WEST LONDON

Park

Harlesden

WILLESDEN JUNCTION

KENSAL RISE JUNC.

WEST LONDON BRANCH

0m 55c

0m 30c 8

0m 30c GOODS

HIGH LEVEL

PASS LOW LEVEL

23c

5c

5c N. & S.W. JUNC.

MITRE BRIDGE JR.

0m 42c

W. LONDON JR.

16c

0m 21c

Wormwood Scrubbs

Prison

County

County

0m 48c

0m 29c

0m 26c

GAFFIN'S SID.

OLD OAK COMS. GOODS DEPOT

5c SID.

17c

OLD OAK LANE

OLD OAK HALT

0m 25c

JUNC. FOR HIGH WYCOMBE

13c

Golf

Course of

M

1 in 13c

1 in 0c

0m 39c

OLD OAK JUNC.

ACTON WELLS JUNCTION

L. & N.W. & N. & S.W. JR.

G.W. & N. & S.W. JR.

0m 28c

Wr. JUNC. JNT.

1 in 3c

W. JUNC. JNT.

1 in 3c

HARLESDEN FOR WEST WILLESDEN & STONEBRIDGE PARK GOODS

0m 28c

2c

METROPOLITAN ELECTRIC SUPPLY CO SW SIDING

1 in 4c

5c

6c

8c

0m 8c

ACTO'G STA.

0m 36c

0m 43c

E & PRICES SID.

1 in 17c

Right
One of the remaining manual signal-boxes in the area is Kensal Green Junction Box, seen here on 5 November 1984. The box is actually situated at the point marked 'Kensal Rise Junc' on the map shown opposite. Its life is nearly over, and may have finished by the time you read these words. What will become of those delightful finials? What, too, will happen to those red, white, yellow and green levers? And to the cast-iron lever identification plates that I photographed – 'To Kensington', 'To New Line', 'Up City Line', 'Up Kensington'?

Left
The Railway Clearing House coloured maps are splendid, decorative, historic and most useful. This extract from the 1913 'OFFICIAL RAILWAY MAP OF LONDON AND ITS ENVIRONS' clearly illustrates the strategic position of Willesden Junction, although by this date the LNWR ('L&NW') owned most of the railway in the immediate vicinity; it is coloured red. Note the West London Joint running south from North Pole Junction (red and yellow); the N & S. Wn. Junc. Jnt running in to Willesden Junction to join the LNWR main line (purple): the Midland line (green) bearing away at Acton Wells Junction to cross the LNWR main line near Harlesden Station: the High Level and Low Level passenger stations at Willesden Junction, described in this chapter.

which now seems an eternity ago, is a church. An examination of my original photographs at least gave me a marker. Even that landmark has now been occluded by a modern industrial structure, but with modern lenses, even in poor light, I have been able to create one 'then and now' feature.

Of the motive power comparisons, there could be few greater contrasts, accentuated by the paraphernalia of the overhead electric-traction equipment. For the first but not the last time that day my stomach lurched with regret at the opportunities missed, gone for ever. Willesden Junction in the steam era, with modern films and cameras, long lenses, and trackside photographic permission would, quite simply, be paradise on earth. One can only but imagine what joyous sights would have been presented to one's lens. To write such words, to think such thoughts is but an extreme form of sado-masochism.

With Ivor at my side, understandably fretting as I photographed electric locomotive-hauled expresses whistling past my ear at 100 m.p.h., we explored the site of the old station. He pointed out the bricked-up wall where once had been the footbridge from the booking-office – still there, serving the High Level station – which spanned the main-line tracks, and from which steps descended to the main line platforms. Whilst

probably few mourn the passing of that dank, depressing old station, which was more LNWR than LMS, its disappearance was, for me, yet another reminder of the near-total extinction of the steam-era Willesden.

Our next move was to the site of the old shed – 1A of renown to railwaymen and enthusiasts alike. Of it, there is no trace whatsoever. It has long since been totally and utterly obliterated, by acres of tarmac associated with the new Freightliner terminal, which merits no more mention than these words.

From this bleak place, I could not depart too rapidly. We returned, under Old Oak Lane, back past the site of Willesden Junction Main Line Station, and clambered up from the track-side to the High Level station, on the Broad Street–Richmond line (I hope, forlornly, that the maps and charts explain the geography of this bewildering place). Called HL in the current Working Timetable, this station (on the former North London Railway) still boasts upper-quadrant semaphore signals. With electrified third-rail, great care is needed when walking the tracks. Immediately to the north of the high-level station, that is, for trains travelling towards Broad Street, the track crosses the 'new lines' of the former LNWR's Watford–Euston (electrified) service. As one looks down from the North London line on to the

By 23 June 1963, some of the lightweight BR Standard '2' 2–6–0's had been allocated to Willesden Shed. No. 78043 (*left*), formerly an Aintree engine, was active in the marshalling yards parallel to and between the main line and the shed. These locomotives were, I think, the last 'new' class deliberately to be allocated to Willesden for specific duties, and 15 were thus deployed between May '63 and June '65, coming from sheds as near as Watford and as far as Bangor, Workington, Chester, Wigan and Widnes. Note the church in the background, perhaps the most obvious landmark to feature in a 'then and now' comparison.

The flattened top (*right*) is more distinctive than the traditional pointed spire and, modern developments notwithstanding, the long lens and the overhead electrification perhaps add dramatic effect to the enlargement of a purely incidental feature in the previous picture.

LNWR, a nameless junction throws a spur off to the left. This spur runs up to Kensal Green Junction, to join the NL tracks from High Level Station, and is used only by two peak-hour services daily. From here is visible the now long-disused sub-station for the DC lines. Ivor and I walked from the High Level station, round the curve towards Kensal Green Junction box, passing under Harrow Road, by bridge 16. On our left, the City Goods Line – a direct freight-only link from the LNWR main line to the NL line to the city – joins the NL line just to the east of the spur referred to above.

The temptation to play at cartography and to produce a series of diagrams is almost as great as the urge to become an amateur railway historian, so perhaps I should resist both temptations. We walked to, and visited, Kensal Green Junction signal-box, itself due to be taken out of service ere long. The box contained numerous LNWR and LMS items, still very much in use, but the day of our visit was notable for seeing the first movement of 'new' electric stock which will replace the London Midland Region electric stock introduced in 1957 and still, at the time of writing, the staple motive power on the Watford–Euston and Richmond–Broad Street services. The irony is that, between the writing of these words and their publication, this stock, very

79

Above left
Their official designation is, I
believe, London Midland
Region London District
Three-Car Sets. They have
been a familiar, if unloved
sight, for many years on the
Watford–Euston and
Richmond–Broad Street
trains, but their days are
numbered too. Indeed they
are, for e.m.u. *aficionados*,
almost ancient. They have
been a familiar sight at both
High Level and Low Level
Willesden stations for more
than a generation, and
presumably someone will
bemoan their passing: albeit
not the passengers, I suspect.

In grisly light for colour
photography, an e.m.u.
bound for Richmond
trundles under a bridge off
the Harrow Road, past a fine
semaphore gantry. It takes
the line which climbs up to
Willesden High Level
Station. The splitting signal's
other arms protect the
junction to the City Goods
line, and to the City Link
loop, which runs down onto
the new lines, below the
High Level Station, and into
Willesden New Station. The
three lines form Kensal Rise
Junction in the map on page
76.

Below left
Location not locomotive is
the reason for including this
shot, of a diesel-hauled train
climbing up the City Goods
Line towards Kensal Rise
Junction (see map on page 76,
section marked $0^m 55^c$), on
my 'return to Willesden' on 5
November 1984. The
strategic importance,
complexity of operation and
variety of motive power –
within today's strict confines
– remains a feature of this

place. No apology is offered for my failure to recognise the 'class' of diesel, if such a word be appropriate for such boxes on wheels, nor for not recording the number of the groaning machine. In the train are some of the Class 313 units, from the Great Northern electrified line and based at Hornsey, which will replace the London District Three-Car compartment sets (501's) introduced nearly 30 years ago, one of which is seen above left.

Right
Having illustrated on page 68 the map covered by section 'CB' of the London Midland Region Working Timetable, this extract from the timetable itself further emphasises Willesden's vital inter-regional pivotal position. Covering three BR regions in such a small time-and-mileage parameter makes this an unusual extraction from a working timetable. On page 83, I refer to the 12.54 train from Brighton to Manchester Piccadilly – 1M07 – which is included at the bottom right of this illustration; it does not actually touch Willesden, running Clapham Junction – Kensington Olympia – North Pole Junction – Old Oak Common East, as the cross-London portion of its journey.

WEEKDAYS CB83 — WILLESDEN TO CLAPHAM JUNCTION

CB82 WEEKDAYS — DOWN — WILLESDEN TO CLAPHAM JUNCTION

Mileage M.C	Station		Col 1	Col 2
			0M08	1052
			01.21LD from Stratford T.M.D	22.30 FO Manchester Piccadilly to Poole
	Willesden Brent Sidings	dep		
0.00	WILLESDEN WEST LONDON JN			
0.36	WILLESDEN WEST LONDON JN			
	Willesden Jn H.L Jn			
	Mitre Bridge Jn	arr		
	Mitre Bridge Jn	dep		
0.73	Old Oak Common East			
	North Pole Jn			
2.63	KENSINGTON OLYMPIA	arr		
	KENSINGTON OLYMPIA	dep		
5.51	Latchmere Jn			
6.24	CLAPHAM JUNCTION	arr		
	CLAPHAM JUNCTION	dep		

WEEKDAYS — CLAPHAM JUNCTION TO WILLESDEN

WEEKDAYS — UP — CLAPHAM JUNCTION TO WILLESDEN

Mileage M.C	Station			
0.00	CLAPHAM JUNCTION	arr		
	CLAPHAM JUNCTION	dep		
0.53	Latchmere Jn			
3.51	KENSINGTON OLYMPIA	arr		
	KENSINGTON OLYMPIA	dep		
5.41	North Pole Jn			
5.68	Old Oak Common East			
0.00	Mitre Bridge Jn	arr		
	Mitre Bridge Jn	dep		
0.35	Willesden Jn H.L Jn			
6.24	WILLESDEN WEST LONDON JN			
	WILLESDEN WEST LONDON JN			

much in use in 1963–65 when last I was photographing (steam) at Willesden, will itself soon be redundant and scrapped. Who will bother to record its passing? Broad Street has gone, too.

Having begun, now, to appreciate the geography of this section of Willesden Junction, Ivor and I set off again on our travels. We walked back, under bridge 16 again, but this time on the City Goods line. The gradient is steep here, as was evidenced by a diesel struggling up the grade with a heavy freight train. At the foot of the grade, we crossed over the tracks again and made for the litter-strewn Low Level Station, known variously as Willesden DC, Willesden Low Level or Willesden New! We also visited the station signal-box, in which were two ex-Great Western men who had found themselves unwillingly transferred from Western to London Midland Region territory some years previously. They commented, as a matter of fact and without rancour, that their new 'employers', the 'Midland', and their new environment, bore no comparison with, and lacked the esprit de corps, of the Great Western world from which they had been peremptorily removed. But that tale is not for this chapter.

Our next destination was the electric MTD, which held no interest for me. However, it was beside the main line, at the most southerly point we had yet reached. From here, we were opposite yet another junction, which Ivor informed me was West London Junction. Before crossing the main lines again, we glanced curiously at a two-car electric unit, No. 6319, transferred from the Southern Region for crew training on the NLR Richmond–Woolwich service, the latter now fully electrified. Of more interest was the former British Transport Hotels (BTH) laundry, recently made redundant.

From West London Junction we walked the track towards Mitre Bridge Junction, passing en route a weird, truncated, short-armed upper-quadrant semaphore signal, which controls southbound trains approaching Mitre Bridge Junction from West London Junction. The relief Signalman on duty in Mitre Bridge Junction Box described this signal as 'Willesden No. 2'.

The proximity of the bridge carrying the West London line over the GWR main line at Old Oak was too tempting to miss, so in spite of Ivor's mild admonition that, once across the Grand Union Canal we were 'no longer really at Willesden Junction' – a point about which there was no dispute – I set up my camera on the girder-bridge; if only, if only I had known about this place, and could have been here in the steam era. What a magnificent location, with an unparalleled view of Old Oak approaches.

From here it was but a step to the top of the bank, down at the bottom of which was North Pole Junction Box, visible in the gathering gloom of a winter's afternoon. Looking through my

The railway influence on, in and around Willesden extended beyond the strict confines of Willesden Junction. Under the London Government Act, 1963, Willesden and Wembley were to be merged in the London Borough of Brent. So herein lies the justification for including this photograph. Indeed, Willesden Junction itself was actually outwith the Borough of Willesden. It was 23 December 1963, and the low sun, watery and wan, silhouettes an unidentified LMS '3F' 0–6–0T as it heads south-east out of Brent Yard, the winter sun casting long shadows on a scene that seems an age away. On BR maps and plans, this section is designated as 'Willesden Brent Sidings'.

500 mm lens, down the 1 in 50 grade, the imagination ran riot at the thought of steam-hauled inter-regional and inter-railway freights, and passenger trains, grinding their way up this tree-lined cross-London artery. Brian Haresnape remembers them; I was never so fortunate. Even as we pondered, there hove into view a Class 47 diesel, which disappeared almost as soon as it came into sight at North Pole Junction. It took the right-hand tracks there, which loop round to dive under the West London and join the GWR at West London Junction. In fact, it was a well-filled passenger train which, from the perusal of the Working Timetable, appeared to be 1M07, the 12.54 Brighton to Manchester Piccadilly train, which is routed Clapham Junction–Kensington Olympia–North Pole Junction–Old Oak Common East. What a fascinating place this is: I could have filled this chapter with many more photographs, of then and now.

As we began our trudge back, up to and over the girder-bridge across the GWR, past Mitre Bridge Junction Box, up to West London Junction and back across the LNWR main line, I felt truly satiated with railway history, geography and industrial archaeology. To appreciate, let alone to understand 'the railway' is a gift for which we should be thankful. Steam has gone, and nothing ever will replace it. As long, however, as there is any bull-head

North and South Western (Hampstead and City Junction) Railway

(Incorporation of Company; Formation of Railway from the London and North Western Railway near the Willesden Station on that Line to the East and West India Docks and Birmingham Junction Railway near the Kentish Town Road with a Branch to the North and South Western Junction Railway; Powers to the London and North Western Railway Company and the East and West India Docks and Birmingham Junction Railway Company to subscribe to the proposed Undertaking; Amendment of Acts).

I estimate the expense of the undertaking referred to in the Bill now pending in Parliament under the above mentioned name or short title at the sum of Two hundred and fifty thousand pounds.

Dated this 23rd day of June One thousand eight hundred and fifty three.

£250,000

George Berkley

In *The Guardian* of 11 June 1985, David McKie, kindly referring to me in his Parliamentary sketch column under the heading 'Britain's champion railway buffer', said that I 'was born approximately 100 years too late. He should have been sitting in Parliament in the days when its members were frequently required to scrutinise the plans for some great new railway project, enthusiastically subscribed to, destined to convey eager carriage loads into hitherto inviolate country.'

He is right! However, it was the prospect of freight as much as passenger traffic that attracted support for the North and South Western (Hampstead and City Junction) Railway scheme, the documentation for which was laid before Parliament on 23 June 1853. The line was built and has certainly, like most of Willesden crossroads, stood the test of time.

track, semaphore signals, frilly station canopies, signal-boxes with levers, old bridges and railway artefacts of infinite variety, then there remains immense interest in the railway. At Willesden Junction there is still interest aplenty: I hope you too may feel the urge to explore one of the great landmarks of Britain's railway landscape.

Pre-Grouping

The Urie 'S15' 4–6–0's were amongst my favourite engines. No. 30507 is seen emerging from Winchfield Yard, on the LSWR main line, on 25 September 1963. Although it was only just over twenty years ago, the scene hereabouts today is unrecognisable, for reasons quite apparent, such as semaphore signals and no third rail.

Notwithstanding the Maunsell alterations to the appearance and performance, the ancestry of the Urie engines would be seen – and I believe felt – by those whose sense of railway history at least equipped them with the knowledge of the heritage of these sturdy, simple and reliable pre-grouping machines, still at work well into the 1960s.

30507 spent most of her life allocated to Feltham. Her confident and (for 1963) clean appearance belies the fact that she has but three months life remaining. Note the eight-wheel tender. Withdrawn in December, she was stored for a few weeks at Feltham, then made the melancholy journey to Cohens of Kettering for scrapping.

To quote one's own words is considered vulgar, is usually immodest, and is generally done as a means of justifying one's claims to wisdom and foresight. However, my reason for recalling the last paragraphs of Chapter 6 of *The Call of Steam* is that, when I wrote the words, they determined me to write more, in a future book, about the pre-grouping engines that were still at work into the 1960s. There is no need to repeat verbatim the words used to recall the last photograph that I took, of an LSWR 'M7' tank-engine. However, now is my opportunity further to scour my own records for details of my 'pre-grouping photo captures'.

For those who had neither the desire nor the opportunity, or perhaps were too young, to be photographing steam in its death-throes, it may be pertinent to recall the surprising resilience shown by many veteran steam-engines. When one considers that some of the BR-built GWR-style pannier tanks of 15xx and 16xx class, lasted less than ten years, and that, whilst the last BR Standard '9F' 2–10–0 was not completed until 1960, the first withdrawals of the class commenced in 1964, it is astonishing that some of the Victorian locomotives of the pre-grouping companies were still in BR revenue-earning service, 60, 70 or 80 years after their construction. Odd examples, even more venerable, survived. By no whit could this be attributed to faulty design or poor construction of the post-nationalisation-built engines; indeed, the '9F's were amongst the sturdiest and best engines ever to pound the tracks. It could, however, be taken as an eloquent testimony to the quality of Victorian engineering.

The fate of some of these particularly long-lasting locomotives can sometimes but not always be attributed to special circumstances. The survival of the three Beattie 2–4–0 well-tanks on the Wenford Bridge line in Cornwall has been told sufficiently frequently not to need repetition here. However one might, if one wished to denigrate their longevity, explain their rebuilding and renewal, the fact remains that they were nearly 90 years old when

The tale of the three 'forgotten' Beattie well-tanks that survived in Cornwall for nearly seventy years is well enough known to render its repetition here superfluous. From the arrival of the first of the class at Wadebridge – by sea from Southampton – in May 1893, to the withdrawal of BR Numbers 30585/6/7 in 1962, these engines were synonymous with the Wenford Bridge line. It was with real pleasure and excitement that I met the trio at Nine Elms shed on 25 May 1963 and my thanks to Driver Rickard for bringing them into the open from the back of the shed, for me to photograph. Introduced by the LSWR in 1874, these 2–4–0 well-tanks were amongst the oldest survivors on BR when they were withdrawn, and 30587, seen here, is now part of the National Collection.

Overleaf
The extraordinary tale of 'E4' 0–6–2T No. 32479 is told in the accompanying text. Built in December 1898, originally numbered 479 by the London Brighton and South Coast Railway (LBSCR) and named *Bevendean*, she is seen in steam here on Brighton shed, at the heart of LBSCR country, on 5 May 1963, less than a month away from withdrawal. Is this the last colour photograph of the last surviving Robert J. Billinton Large Radial Tank?

finally withdrawn in 1962. It was with considerable excitement that I photographed these engines at Nine Elms on 25 May 1963. They had been brought to London following their withdrawal in recognition of the fact that their venerable age made them 'collectors' items'.

Strangely, the Southern Region, whose predecessor the Southern Railway had heralded the demise of steam by the widespread introduction of electrification in the 1930s, provided the scenario for the survival of some most unlikely veterans and sometimes circumstances eeked out for them a few extra months or years. The 'E4' 0–6–2T engines were, in terms of overall British locomotive practice and performance, nothing exceptional. That I was able to see three members of the class before they became extinct with the withdrawal of No. 32479 in June 1963, speaks for itself. As ever, I am indebted to *Railway Observer (RO)* the invaluable and irreplaceable monthly magazine of the Railway Correspondence and Travel Society (RCTS) for recording the lingering decline and final demise of these old warriors. Their final weeks are recorded thus, in *RO*, the March 1963 edition of which noted, under the heading 'E4' class:

Continued shortage of power led to a remarkable development on 12th January, when two more engines of the class 32474/9, were resurrected from the dump at Hove and restored to traffic. 32479 is believed to have been sent to Newhaven and was engaged in shunting in Lewes Yard in lieu of a diesel, on 18th January. 32474 went to Three Bridges on the 13th and on several days in the ensuing week was used on the Three Bridges–East Grinstead passenger service, also performing various shunting and local freight duties in the Three Bridges area. On 22nd January it was sent up to Redhill to replace a defective diesel on shunting work there and some days later it was receiving attention on Redhill Shed.

Further to trace the story, the April 1963 edition of *RO* stated:

After several not very active weeks at Redhill, 32474 was sent light to Tunbridge Wells on 16th February, but its stay there was short and it soon found its way back to Three Bridges, where it was seen shunting on 22nd February. On the 26th it was noted passing East Croydon light in the London direction, presumably en route for Norwood. It was shunting at East Croydon the following evening.

32479 and 32503 were still at work in the Brighton area at the end of February.

Left
As ever, coincidence and chance combine to enable me to include this venerable if unremarkable shot of LBSCR 'E4' 0–6–2T No. 479 *Bevendean* taken in the early years of this century. Notwithstanding a rather poor photograph – bunker out of focus – the engine is obviously gleaming inside and out. Its inclusion here is for the fun of comparison with BR No. 32479 on pages 90 and 91: the same locomotive, of course. For its use, I am indebted to the Locomotive Publishing Co, courtesy of Ian Allan Ltd. In particular, I thank David Allan and Simon Forty for their flexibility in breaking their own rules about using their library pictures in other publishers' books: long live flexible publishers!

In the June 1963 *RO*, 32503 (75A) is shown in the list of April withdrawals, and under the heading 'Brighton' there appears:

32503 ran light to Eastleigh for scrap on 13th April, leaving 32479 as the sole surviving 'E4' in this area.

32479 itself is listed under the May withdrawals in the July edition of *RO*, which contains the following paragraph, again under the heading of 'E4' class:

Norwood's 32474 left light on its final journey to Eastleigh on 11th May. It had continued in regular work up to the previous day when it was noted heading the 1.44 p.m. New Cross Gate–Norwood freight. The last of the Billinton Radials to remain at work was thus 32479 at Newhaven, where it had for sometime been deputising for a shunting diesel; it was so employed on 19th May but this appears to have been its final duty and by the next day it had been sent to Brighton and was said to be awaiting the summons to Eastleigh, or banishment to the dump at Hove.

The end of the story, sadly but inevitably, is dutifully recorded in the August 1963 *RO*, which, in the listing of 'Withdrawals' notes under June: '0–6–2T "E4" 32479[†]' that dreaded dagger, like a small sword; then, below, '[†]last of class'.
The copy then closes the life of these Victorian veterans thus:

Right
Introduced by L. B. Billinton in 1913, the seventeen 'K' class 2–6–0's were the maids-of-all-work on the freight services of LBSCR, then SR and then of BR Southern Region up to the date of their withdrawal. In the background is an even more ancient LBSCR machine – 'E6' 0–6–2T No. 32417, built in 1905 and itself one of the last three to survive until December 1962. Seen here at Brighton shed on 5 May 1963, 'K' No. 32342 has her motion partly removed, as both locomotives are moved by a diesel shunter. Note the water-column in the background; and beyond that, the Southern Region green of the day.

'E4' class – Last survivor of the LBSC 'Radials' in traffic on BR, 32479 left Brighton light for Eastleigh on 1st June. 32468, withdrawn earlier in the year, was booked to be hauled dead from Brighton to Eastleigh on 29th June, together with 30923.

Further perusal of subsequent *RO*'s would indicate the date of the cutting-up of each individual engine, but this exercise becomes too morbid. At the going down of the sun, we shall remember them . . .

Extensive quotation is not only painful, it lays me open to the charge of laziness and lack of imagination. This book, like its predecessors, however, is a purely personal record of remembrance. In August 1965, more than two years after the demise of the 'E4's', I found myself at St Margaret's Shed, in Edinburgh, surveying an even older class of Victoriana. By this date, 19th-century steam was becoming distinctly rare. In Scotland, the last Caledonian engine had gone by 1963, but nine of the 168 North British class 'J36' 0—6—0s, with 5ft 0in wheels, were still listed as in service in the Ian Allan *Locoshed Book*, updated for the Scottish Region to 24 April 1965. One of these survivors of a class built between 1888 and 1900, was No. 65234, still in use, albeit as stationary boiler, at St Margaret's Shed when I visited.

Only at the final stage of completing the text for this book did there occur one of those strange coincidences which so enrich my life, and for which one is so grateful. The occasion was a committee meeting of the National Railway Museum, being held on the premises of its 'parent', the Science Museum in South Kensington. Somehow during the meeting there arose some discussion on the maintenance, storage or display of historic documents. It was either Dr John Coiley or Tony Hall-Patch who mentioned, *en passant*, that a quantity of the original working drawings from the North British Locomotive Company (NBL) had been presented to the Museum when the Glasgow works closed down. My ears pricked up: as soon as was decent after the meeting, I cajoled Tony Hall-Patch to let me inspect some of this — to me unknown — treasure-trove.

To say that it was uncatalogued, and its precise extent unknown, is not intended as any criticism. The vast, seemingly limitless quantity of early railway documentation constantly being unearthed and donated to the museums is a subject way outwith the scope of this book. However, with Tony's enthusiastic help we groped our way through sheets of hand-written documentation. There are gems indeed here. Among the NBL's constituent companies were Dübs, Nielson, Nielson Reid and Sharp Stewart. Carefully stored are beautiful hand-tinted working drawings of a wide variety of locomotives, built for railways as diverse as the South-Eastern and Chatham, the Midland, and the Glasgow and South-Western, not to mention the North British Railway, and innumerable overseas customers around the globe. As this information is being inserted into this chapter at a very late stage, let it suffice that I spotted an opportunity to

By 5 August 1965, there were precious few North British Railway (NBR) locomotives left. Albeit by now reduced to the status of stationary boiler, former NBR Class 'C' (No. 658), subsequently LNER Class 'J36' 0-6-0 No. 65234, built at Carstairs in July 1891, certainly earns her place here. She is seen at Edinburgh St Margaret's shed. These Holmes locomotives, the first of which appeared in 1888, totalled 168 by the time the last was built, in 1900. No. 65234 was in use as stationary boiler at St Margaret's until July 1967, by which date she was exactly 76 years old. Prior to transfer to St Margaret's in September 1964, No. 65234 had been a Bathgate engine for some years.

Note the oval patch of rust on the splasher, where was the manufacturer's plate.

The story of how I 'found' this item for inclusion is told on this page. My thanks to Tony Hall-Patch, and acknowledgements to the Science Museum, for what is probably another 'first': the reproduction in colour of an original Sharp Stewart & Co working drawing juxtaposed, above, with a colour photograph of a locomotive of the same class. The Sharp Stewart batch were all built for the NBR in early 1892, just six months after 65234. Their NBR numbers were 678–92.

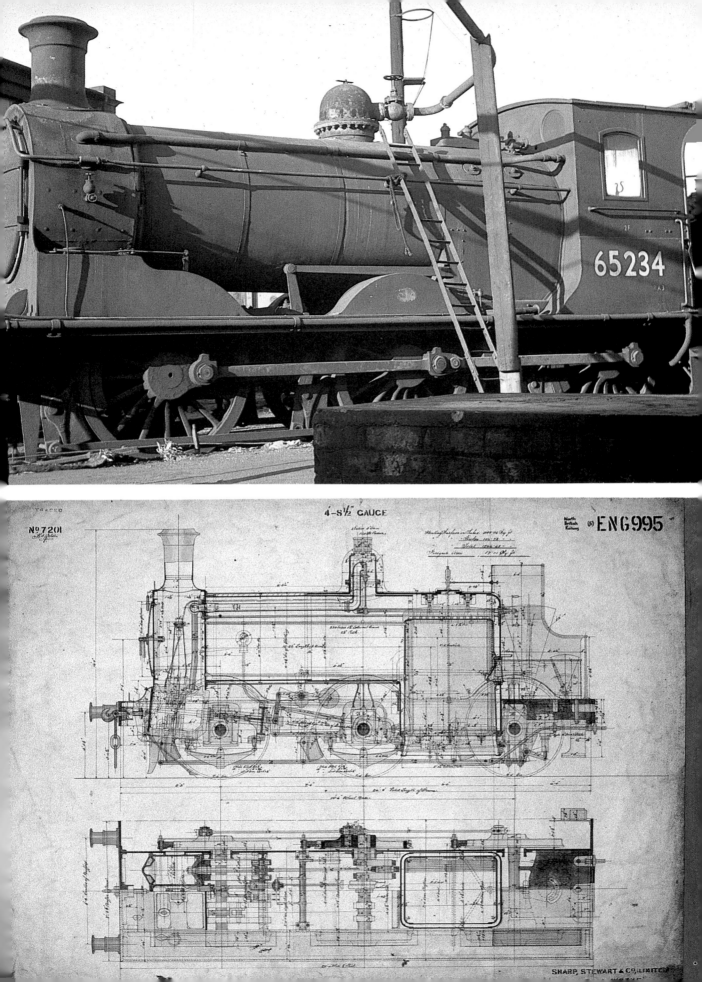

juxtapose a working drawing, in colour, alongside one of my colour photographs of the same class of locomotive. Thus, here is reproduced a (rather cramped and inadequate) photograph of that Holmes North British 'J36', No. 65234, built in 1891; and a working drawing, in colour too, of one of the same class of locomotives built the following year by Neilson & Co: surely a unique juxtaposition for colour publication. (See page 95.)

These recollections, so carefully documented by *Railway Observer* for enthusiasts, highlight the intense interest in the veterans of steam that relate to this chapter's title. Visiting a shed was, for an enthusiast, rather like the anticipation of a philatelist presented with a box of assorted stamps. For us, an 'E4', a 'J36', an Aspinall L & Y Class '21' or a GWR 'Star' were akin to a Cape of Good Hope Triangular: yet unlike the philatelic analogy, our interest was untinged with anticipation of financial gain. Our nostalgic feelings, too, were more than just 'interest'. We loved these engines. Again, unlike the stamps, they have gone. In fact, my philatelic analogy is really not too close. Stamps never lived.

At the start of this chapter I confessed that my personal recollections of the 'M7' class, comprising the chapter under that title in a previous book, motivated me to write this one. How strange it is, and how utterly incomprehensible it must be to non-enthusiasts to realise the painful pleasure obtained by detailed study of the life – and death, usually – of each individual engine. What strangely morbid curiosity leads me, these 20 years later, to resurrect my old hand-written catalogue, then to do likewise to my fading copies of old magazines? Yet I can only assume, and certainly hope, that this exercise rings a bell with you, too.

It is unnecessary for me to repeat my apologies that I am no historian. Memory, anecdote and inadequate photographs are all that is in my possession. Each chapter written leads to further examination of my records, and this act of examination is itself sufficient to realise and to appreciate the unplumbed depths of railway interest contained within those seemingly-turgid lists of facts and figures. I had contemplated ending this chapter by listing the photographs of pre-grouping locomotives taken. After two hours and the expenditure of time plus lead on paper, I gave up, because there were so many.

Perhaps one day I may be able to prove the insatiable and fanatical appetite of railway enthusiasts by producing, in book form, the list of photographs I took as an end in itself; a catalogue in praise of steam. Are any publishers reading this book?

Immodesty encourages me to invite you to read my chapter on the 'M7' in *The Call of Steam*. These Drummond 0–4–4 tanks, introduced on the LSWR in 1897, eventually wandered far and wide across the Southern Railway, but Nine Elms must have seemed a spiritual home. By May 1964 just nine members of the class remained in service, one of which was No. 30053. All were withdrawn that month. I was therefore fortunate to find this engine still at Nine Elms on 7 July that year, two days after hauling the 'Surrey Wanderer' rail tour through the Home Counties; 30053 was the last active Drummond engine, although officially already withdrawn. After this, she was removed to Eastleigh Works for restoration and export to the USA, where she still resides, doubtless not really appreciated. Behind the 'M7' is a stranger – GWR '57xx' 0–6–0PT No. 4672. This was one of the Pannier Tanks transferred to Nine Elms for use on empty stock workings from Waterloo. 4672 went to Nine Elms, from Cardiff (Radyr) in January 1959, and was withdrawn in July 1963. She was stored firstly at Feltham; then back at Nine Elms for most of 1964 before being scrapped at Wards, Briton Ferry in December that year, albeit only 20 years old – a modest age for GWR locomotives.

Midland Railway 0–6–0 tanks and their LMS successors cannot claim to be amongst the most exciting or rare locomotives, yet even the comparatively modern 'Jinty' – a word I dislike – was becoming photographically desirable as steam approached its final five years. From an earlier era, and distinctive with its condensing apparatus – fitted to engines working in the London area – is Johnson large Midland design '3F' 0–6–0T No. 47202, seen here near Brent Junction, Cricklewood on 6 April 1963. For many years a Kentish Town locomotive, she was allocated to Cricklewood MPD from August 1962 to October 1963. As luck would have it, and thanks only to P. B. Hands' *What Happened to Steam*, I discover that 47202 was one of the last two ultimate survivors, in December 1966, of a class introduced by the Midland Railway in 1899.

Note the then-new Austin 'Cambridge' or Morris 'Oxford' on the car-flats: if any of them last in service for 67 years it would be a miracle! 47202 had been transferred to Cricklewood from Kentish Town when the latter lost its steam allocation about the time I started my railway photography.

Condenser-fitted locos, for use on the 'Widened Lines' were based at Kentish Town for many years. It was often said that the apparatus was more cosmetic than useful, although officialdom would doubtless have denied this.

6   2–6–4T

Have you noticed how journalists always seek a suitable adjective with which to describe people and things? An actress is 'sultry' or 'glamorous' or 'brilliant'; a lorry-driver is 'burly' or 'long distance' or 'experienced'. In recent years, changing styles of railway journalism have sought to introduce this technique to our particular field of interest. Thus we have a 'sleek' 'A4' or a 'fussy' Pannier-tank or a 'workmanlike' 'Black 5'. This language is now welded on to the traditional image of individual classes and wheel-arrangements of locomotives. Almost all classes and groups have thus been categorised – and there is nothing wrong with that. Yet for some reason, either my reading has denied me access to, or there has not been much railway literature devoted to, the 2–6–4 tank engine as such.

Wheel arrangements started with 'Rocket' and contemporaries, when four wheels on an 'engine' and four wheels on a 'tender' seemed the obvious answer to what are now considered 'primitive' machines. If one were to trace the evolution of the wheel arrangement – as such – on British steam engines, it would I think become apparent that the 2–6–4T was very late on the scene. A few speculative thoughts on the reasons for this may expose my ignorance, but satisfy my inquisitiveness.

As any budding toy or model railway enthusiast will recall, the 0–4–0 is usually the 'nursery' wheel arrangement, graduating to 0–6–0. Bogies come off rails more easily than driving-wheels. Thus in the early years, driving wheels sufficed – bogies did not exist. What applies to the nursery toy, applied to the real steam-engine in its childhood, vide Trevithick, Stephenson *et al.* As the state of the art advanced, and as quality of track improved, traffic-requirements became more sophisticated and as the added weight and length of locomotives had to be negotiated round curves, the bogie emerged as the answer.

The first British standard-gauge 2–6–4T was the Robinson Great Central 'IB' class (later LNER Class 'L1', then reclassified

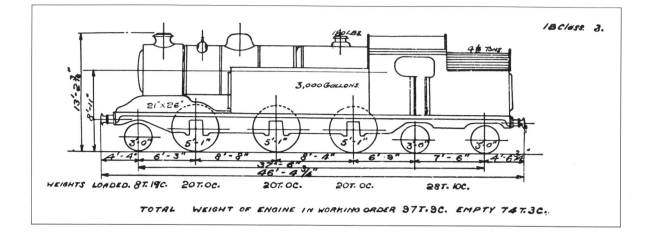

'L3'), twenty of which were built between 1914 and 1917. (Two earlier narrow-gauge 2–6–4T engines ran on the Leek and Manifold Railway). Like their ill-fated SR successors, the 'River' Tanks – more of which later – the Great Central locomotives quickly acquired a reputation for rolling, earning them the nickname 'Crabs' from the enginemen. They could hardly have been less like the Hughes-Fowler 2–6–0s of similar nickname insofar as their stability, reliability, popularity and suitability was concerned. Originally intended by the GCR for the coal traffic from the Nottinghamshire and Derbyshire coalfield, to Immingham for export, their mechanical unsuitability made them early candidates for transfer. Before the grouping they wandered around the Great Central sheds, some at Gorton, some at Annesley, some at Woodford. On trip freights, occasional local passenger services, and banking or piloting duties they were never spectacular; the most 'spectacular' event was probably when one lost control of a train descending from Woodhead and ended up in the sand at Hadfield.

After the Grouping, and reclassified Class 'L1', the LNER made the most of this class of fairly lame ducks, but again mostly on shunting, marshalling and banking duties. One engine, LNER No. 5272 at Retford, earned itself the nickname 'The Zeppelin' which name spread. Some of the class were shedded for some years at Neasden, where one lightweight duty involving three reversals make a tank-engine suitable. Their greatest use on passenger trains followed the opening of Wembley Stadium loop-line, when on the occasion of special sporting events, numerous trains ran to and from Marylebone, and Neasden thus found a use for its 'L1' tanks.

Lest I turn this chapter into an operational case-history of each class of 2–6–4T, I shall finish the saga of the 'L1's by mentioning

Due to the vagaries of British Rail's system for collation, storage and restoration of the literally innumerable historic drawings, plans, charts, maps and documents, it is to the office of Dennis Rowell, Regional Civil Engineer at Paddington, that my thanks are directed for permission to reproduce this outline drawing of the first British Standard Gauge 2–6–4 tank: Great Central Class '1B' (see this page).

Nobody seems really to know why these, and the other three drawings in this chapter, came to be at Paddington. However, to Dave Faulkner and his colleagues my thanks for making available material that makes up for the obvious gap in my photography.

From the few photographs I have seen of these GCR 2–6–4 tanks, the drawing was more handsome than the end-product. Indeed, their bulky and portentous appearance seemed quite unlike the clean-cut and business-like aspect which characterised most, if not all, the post-grouping classes of this wheel-arrangement. Unlike later engines, however, these Great Central '1B' 2–6–4 tanks were designed for short-haul coal traffic, for which task good acceleration was presumably not a priority.

only that the first of the class was withdrawn in July 1947, and thereafter scrapping continued. Perhaps it is surprising, in view of their inadequacies, that they lasted as long as they did. The penultimate withdrawal of the by-then-reclassified 'L3's, now BR No. 69050, the first of the class, built in 1914, took place in March 1955; and the last of the class, BR No. 69069, went in July the same year, although it served as stationary boiler at Stratford Carriage Works until September 1957 when it was finally cut up.

They were ugly engines; to me the adjectives 'bulky' or 'constipated' seem appropriate. On the introduction of Thompson's new class of 'L1' 2–6–4T in 1945, the old GCR engines were – as mentioned above – redesignated as Class 'L3'. In order to stick to chronology I shall refer to the Thompson 'L1's in a moment, because a passing mention must be made of another class, the LNER 'L2' 2–6–4T, formerly Metropolitan Railway Class 'K', of which six were built, by Armstrong Whitworth in 1925. Not only were they the last engines built for the Metropolitan, they had a fascinating link with R. E. L. Maunsell's 'River' tanks. Indeed, it was only during my research for this chapter, and due mainly to the informative and excellent RCTS series 'Locomotives of the LNER' that I learned of the link, details of which are also provided by Brian Haresnape in his *Maunsell Locomotives*.

Readers of *In Search of Steam* may recall, and you will doubtless anyway be familiar with the SECR 'Woolworths', the 'N' class 2–6–0s, the first of which emanated from Woolwich Arsenal during the First World War. Anyway, as they say, the story goes thus: when the Arsenal's programme was complete, the Cohen and Armstrong Disposal Corporation bought the parts for the 'K' class 2–6–4Ts. George Hally CME of the Metropolitan, designed the engines, the tapered boilers for which, built by Robert Stephenson & Co, certainly added to the Maunsell-like appearance.

All six Metropolitan-designed, London Transport-acquired, and finally LNER engines, spent their lives at the GCR/LNER Neasden depot, whence most of their working hours were allocated to the Metropolitan's suburban freight services between Verney Junction and Finchley Road. Not only were they similar to the SR 'River' class tanks, both were, coincidentally, designated Class 'K'. If anything, they were more handsome than the erstwhile and ill-fated Southern engines; they had 5ft 6in rather than 6ft 0in driving wheels and the longer bunkers gave a sleeker, less 'high-riding' look. Undoubtedly they were safer . . . although this may be a slightly unfair comment, as the Metropolitan 'K's were used on freight rather than express passenger trains, until the LNER took them over with their acquisition of

the steam operations of the Metropolitan in 1937. Their new owners put them to work on passenger trains, at which work they proved most capable.

Not much is written about these six locomotives, although they are discussed, as mentioned, with good illustration, in Brian Haresnape's excellent *Maunsell Locomotives*, thus confirming their heritage. What a great pity that the LNER scrapped them; the first was withdrawn in January 1943. Two of the class survived until 1948 to become BR engines, but before the year was out they too were withdrawn, without being renumbered. Had they been offered to the Southern by the LNER, they could have joined a substantial Maunsell locomotive fleet, albeit years after the 'Rivers' on the SR had been converted to 'U' class Moguls in 1928. But, with the memory of the 'Rivers', would the Southern have accepted such a gift, had it ever been made? I doubt it.

In order to resist the temptation to be repetitive, yet to do justice to their role in the saga of the British 2—6—4 tank engine, mention must be made of the tragedy and controversy of Maunsell's 'K' Class River Tanks. The first of the class, No. 790, appeared in June 1917 from the SECRs Ashford Works. It actually preceded the prototype 'N' class 'Mogul' referred to above, of which it was the tank-engine version. The wheel-arrangement was not common, and I do not know what if any

Fairburn 2—6—4T No. 42086 stands at signals in Luton Midland Road Station, on a murky winter's day in November 1962. This indeed was one of my very first photographs and few scenes could better illustrate the transition in the working main-line railway then and now. Electrification, and rationalisation – the smart word for decimation – of freight services, have utterly transformed Luton.

No apology is offered for including such a workaday scene, as this epitomises the steam era in its closing years. 42086 was a representative of the final manifestation of LMS engines of this wheel-arrangement. A Cricklewood engine at this date, she finished her days at Birkenhead, from which shed withdrawal occurred in April 1967. The immediate numerical predecessor 42085 is preserved at the Lakeside and Haverthwaite Railway.

inspiration or cognisance Maunsell had, of the Robinson Great Central '1B' locomotives, already referred to. There was a gap of eight years between the appearance of the prototype No. 790, and the order – by now by the SR – of the main batch of these engines; numbers A791–A809 being built in 1925/6. The SR actually placed the orders only after thorough tests on No. 790, and due to pressure of work at Ashford, nine sets of parts were sent to Armstrong Whitworth, and ten sets to Brighton. The final engine was redesigned by Maunsell as a three-cylinder 2–6–4T and classified 'K1'; it was even less stable than the two-cylinder 'K's, in spite of its bulk and attractive appearance. It was numbered A890 and named *River Frome*.

On 27 March 1927 A890's leading coupled wheels derailed at Wrotham, Kent. As a result, all the 'Rivers' were kept off the Maidstone line until July. No sooner were they reinstated to traffic than No. A800 was derailed at Maidstone East. Then No. A890 was again derailed; between Bearstead and Hollingbourne; seven coaches of the train left the track. Finally, and disastrously for the whole class of 2–6–4Ts, came the infamous Sevenoaks tragedy. On 24 August 1927 No. A800 *River Cray*, travelling at speed at the head of the 5 p.m. Pullman Car Express from Cannon Street to Deal, plunged off the road near the Shoreham Lane overbridge at Sevenoaks. Several carriages were flung against the abutments of the bridge. Thirteen people were killed, 40 badly injured, and drastic and immediate action was taken by the Southern. By 8 p.m. that night, all the 'River' tanks were confined to their sheds. The fate of the class was sealed.

In spite of subsequent high-speed tests on a piece of prime LNER main line, and further tests on the SR, the whole class of 21 tanks was withdrawn and converted to 2–6–0s. As such the 'U' Moguls – more of which were built later, as class 'U' with only detailed alterations from the converts – subsequently served SR and BR Southern Region faithfully for many years. Yet Maunsell was not to be daunted or inalienably prejudiced against the 2–6–4T wheel-arrangement. Nor did he wish unnecessarily to waste the side-tanks and bogies, discarded when the 'Rivers' were converted to tender engines. In response to a particular need of the SR – sturdy tank engines for transfer freight purposes in the London area, with good acceleration and good braking – he designed a new class, the 'W' 2–6–4T, with completely new features to overcome the weaknesses of the 'Rivers'.

Fifteen 'W' class engines were built, at Eastleigh and Ashford. The first five emerged from Eastleigh in 1932, and the remaining ten during 1935/36 from Ashford. Their careers could hardly have been more markedly different from their ill-fated co-wheel-arrangement forerunners. Even down to their numbers, they

Overleaf
Transferred to Birkenhead (8H) shed from Chester (6A) in June 1965, and with less than a year to live, Stanier taper-boiler 2–6–4T No. 42606 pounds up the grade past the entrance to Mollington Street Shed, Birkenhead, with the 2.55 p.m. Birkenhead (Woodside) to Paddington train on 14 November 1965. She will probably come off at Chester.

Note the express passenger lamps; electric warning flash on the leading edge at the top of the tank; semaphore signals; driver leaning out of his cab; and the deplorable state of the locomotive on a line in its dying days. The first through train ran from Paddington to Birkenhead on 10 October 1861; the last on 5 March 1967.

To contemplate the fate of the railway in this photograph is but painfully to remember how the old company rivalries ended. The GWR route from Merseyside to London is extinct. Birkenhead Woodside is no more, and the second-class-only service from Rock Ferry to Chester is but an insult to the memory of a main line.

Only 15 in number, and somewhat camera-shy, few colour photographs of Maunsell's 'W' class 2–6–4T seem to have been published. Developed from the 'N1' 2–6–0s, these locomotives spent most of their lives on transfer freight work in the London area. Norwood Junction MPD (75C) was a shed that I never visited but it always had an allocation of 'W' tanks, of which No. 31919 was one. It is seen here on shed at Three Bridges on 16 April 1963, with steam to spare.

Of the 15 engines, 10 were withdrawn in 1963, and the remaining five in the following years. Sadly, none survived into preservation. One can only surmise whether, were it not for the saga of the 'River' tanks, any of these handsome engines would have been used on passenger trains.
As with Stanier 2–6–4T No. 42606 in the previous photograph, there is an electric warning flash on the front of the tank; the 'W's worked through to Willesden, where the commencement of the overhead electrification work on the LNWR main line coincided with the demise of these Maunsell locomotives.

Note the steps alongside the leading driving-wheel; and the water-column. What a wretched state 31919 is in.

were a model of consistency; unlike the other, earlier classes mentioned in this chapter, their original numbers were unaltered, save only for the addition of '3' as the prefix to denote their post-nationalisation status.

Not until the twilight of their lives did they leave the London area, where they had been allocated to Stewarts Lane, Hither Green and Norwood sheds. Typical of their mundane duties were cross-London inter-regional freights, such as Norwood Yard to Willesden Junction. In 1961 two were transferred to Feltham, and more joined them as their date of withdrawal approached. By the beginning of 1964 only five were left, all of which were by then allocated to Feltham. The only ones that 'escaped' the metropolis went to Exmouth Junction Shed, and were used almost exclusively as bankers between Exeter St Davids and Central Stations.

One interesting story involving the 'W's concerns the rumour that O. V. S. Bulleid himself, whilst discussing Brighton Works construction of LMS 2–6–4 tanks just after nationalisation, enquired why the Southern needed to use alien 2–6–4 motive power, when the Region had its own, namely the 'W's. Notwithstanding the lasting memory of the 'Rivers', it is alleged that OVSB insisted on a trial of a 'W' on a passenger-train. There was, it seems, no trouble with stability, but much trouble with a very hot engine . . . and that was the end of a very short-lived experiment. I saw and photographed my first 'W' on shed at Three Bridges, No. 31919, on 16 April 1963, seven months before withdrawal. They were a camera-shy breed and few colour photographs of the class exist. Bulleid, incidentally, was not enamoured of the idea of building LMS '8F's at Brighton either. He considered the design to be old-fashioned and would have preferred a 2–8–0 version of his 'Q'. It would probably have been an excellent engine – but that is another story.

Mention in the last paragraph of the LMS 2–6–4 tanks is the cue for discussing and including in this chapter what transpired to be unquestionably the largest, most successful and genealogically longest-lasting members of the family of this wheel-arrangement. In justification of this claim, by a non-technical author, I propose to consider the Fowler/Stanier/Fairburn/Riddles 2–6–4T's of LMS and BR continuation as members of the same family. To do otherwise would require lengthy and detailed technical explanations outwith both the scope and style of this book. Lest anyone feel that my failure to detail the importance of Stanier's taper-boiler, his three-cylinder engines, changes such as outside steam-pipes – the detailed alterations and improvements are legion – then I can only apologise and refer you to the many excellent books specialising in such information. With my simple

and technically untrained eye, it was the cosmetic rather than the mechanical differences that attracted my attention to the early, Fowler, engines. Both style of chimney, and of smoke-box number plate, were enough to make the remaining Fowler engines an attraction for the camera by the time my photography started.

Historically, the birth of this breed of 2–6–4 tank was a microcosm of the birth of the LMS, and latterly of the locomotive policy of British Railways, and can be summed up in the words 'versatility' and 'standardisation', neither of which particularly denotes excitement, but both of which gladdens the hearts of the operating department. Between them, Fowler, Stanier, Fairburn and the Brighton design office in BR days turned out 800 locomotives precisely (I wonder if anyone else has added up this total of these particular locomotives) and they were undoubtedly sound and successful. The adaptations and changes made over the years improved route availability as well as economy and performance, and the BR class '4' 2–6–4Ts were handsome engines indeed. With the raising of the footplating over the cylinders, and the curved style that was accentuated by BR's lined black livery, the Standard tanks were noticeably more attractive than the Fairburn engines.

Personal choice, not lack of suitable material, accounts for the inclusion of another Fairburn 2—6—4T, rather than one of the BR Standard Class '4' variety, of which a number has survived into preservation. Here, No. 42118 heads a southbound freight at Kensington Olympia in November 1962: another of my early photographs. For many years a Willesden engine, 42118 would doubtless have covered many similar duties to 'W' No. 31919 seen in the previous photograph. Cross-London freights needed reliable motive-power with good acceleration, by the nature of the work.

The importance of this link in the metropolis ensures its existence, and its history is recalled in an earlier chapter, 'This was Willesden'.

To seek to write about their main areas of operation, or to give performance details, is not my intention. Perhaps the most distinctive contribution was made by the Stanier 3-cylinder engines on the Southend line, where they dominated the passenger services for some years. It was generally felt, however, that the 3-cylinder engines gave little extra benefit over and above the 2-cylinder machines, and only 37 were built by Stanier before he reverted to the 2-cylinder version.

Coming into service so soon after the Sevenoaks disaster on the Southern, there must have been some discussion by Fowler of the events which befell the Maunsell 2—6—4Ts. Where Maunsell had failed, Fowler succeeded. Yet the final attempt to design and build a 2—6—4 tank, that of class 'L1' by Thompson for the LNER, was something less than outstandingly successful. The first 'L1' No. 9000 emerged from Doncaster works in May 1945. Extensive trials were conducted and between 1948 and 1950 a further 99 engines of the class were built. Praise was rarely theirs, although some of the approbation may have been due to Thompson's personal unpopularity, particularly with what many people claimed to be his disdain for all things Gresley. Col. H. C. B. Rogers, in his book *Thompson and Peppercorn* sums up what seems to have become the general view. He says (page 95):

> Nobody would claim that the 'L1's were a success. They were temperamental in their steaming and quite unreliable unless carefully handled by crews who knew them. In addition, they were expensive to maintain; the bearing surfaces in the axleboxes were inadequate for the loads they had to bear and wore out rapidly. This wear, combined with the rapid revolution of the small coupled wheels at speed caused wear in the motive parts and connecting rods.

With a tractive effort of 32,080 lb. the 'L1' was easily the most powerful British 2—6—4T, and they were also the last new design, in that the BR standard version was in essence the LMS machine updated. Thompson, by designing and bringing to fruition his 2—6—4 tank, was in fact consummating an idea which had attracted Gresley for many years. Indeed, in 1919, he had wanted to introduce such an engine on the Great Northern Railway, for use on the Metropolitan City widened lines. The Civil Engineer rejected this scheme. Doncaster tried again in 1925: Stratford produced a proposal for yet another 2—6—4T in 1927, intended for the Liverpool Street-Southend services. This scheme met its end, and design work ceased following the demise of *River Cray* at Sevenoaks. (Gresley, incidentally, found nothing inherently wrong with the 'Rivers' . . .)

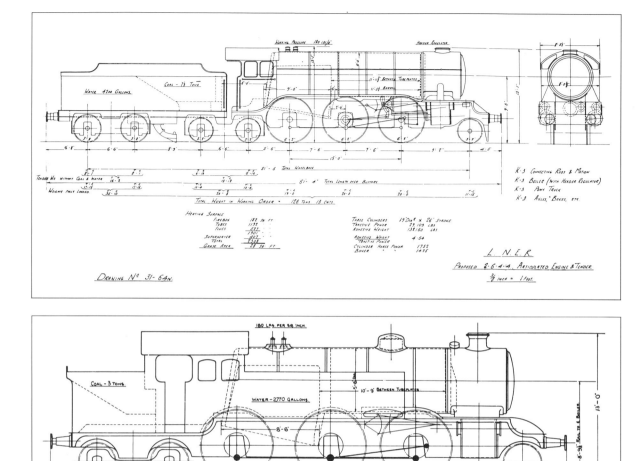

WORKING PRESSURE 180 LBS/□"

HEADER REGULATOR

COAL - 1¾ TONS

WATER 4200 GALLONS

11-1¼ BETWEEN TUBEPLATES
11-1¾ BARREL

9-0"

K-3 CONNECTING RODS & MOTION
K-3 BOILER (WITH HEADER REGULATOR)
K-3 PONY TRUCK
K-3 AXLES, BOXES, ETC

TENDER WT WITHOUT COAL & WATER

WEIGHT FULLY LOADED

51'-5 TOTAL WHEELBASE

51'-4" TOTAL LENGTH OVER BUFFERS

TOTAL WEIGHT IN WORKING ORDER - 126 TONS 13 CWTS

HEATING SURFACE
FIREBOX   182 SQ FT
TUBES   1192
FLUES   527
                 1701
SUPERHEATER   407
TOTAL   2108
GRATE AREA   28 SQ FT

THREE CYLINDERS   19 DIA° X 26" STROKE
TRACTIVE POWER   29,103 LBS
ADHESIVE WEIGHT   138,160 LBS
ADHESIVE WEIGHT   4.54
 TRACTIVE POWER
CYLINDER HORSE POWER 1752
 BOILER   1475

L.N.E.R.

DRAWING N° 31-64N.

PROPOSED 2-6-4-4, ARTICULATED ENGINE & TENDER

⅜ INCH = 1 FOOT.

180 LBS PER SQ INCH.

COAL - 3 TONS

WATER - 2770 GALLONS

10'-9" BETWEEN TUBEPLATES

8-9¼ RAIL TO ⅊ BOILER

13'-0"

8'-6"

6'-2" DIA

3'-5 DIA

2'-5 DIA

4'-3   6'-6   5'-10   8'-2   7'-6   9'-3   5'-10

37'-3" TOTAL WHEELBASE

45'-4" OVER BUFFERS

21-2   18-0   17-0   16-0   13-10

85 TONS, 12 CWT.

2 CYLINDERS, - 20" DIA X 26" STROKE.   TRACTIVE EFFORT - 21,502 LBS.

BOILER.
HEATING SURFACE.
FIREBOX.   - 171.5   SQ. FT.
FLUES.   - 354.53   SQ. FT.
TUBES.   - 871.75   SQ. FT.
TOTAL EVAPORATIVE H.S. - 1397.78   SQ. FT.
SUPERHEATER.   - 246.1   SQ. FT.
TOTAL HEATING SURFACE. - 1643.88   SQ. FT.

GRATE AREA - 26 SQ FT.
BOILER PRESSURE - 180 LBS PER SQ. INCH.

Another link in the thread of the 2–6–4T story, still with the LNER, was the request from the Running Department to Thompson for a locomotive similar to, but an updated version of, the former Metropolitan Railway Class 'K' (LNER Class 'B2') engines. Indeed, it was this request that really fathered the 'L1' Class and ensured its place as one of the ten standard types designed by Thompson to conform to LNER motive power requirements. As the 'mixed traffic tank' in Thompson's menu, the 'L1' was never destined to be, was never likely to be and

Above left
Of the four drawings in this chapter, two are of locomotives that were built, and two of machines that never made it beyond the drawing-board. Undoubtedly the Gresley 2–6–4–4 articulated is the most unusual. For those who would designate this

locomotive as a 2–6–2 with tender, my answer lies at the bottom right-hand corner of this working drawing, where the wording 'LNER Proposed 2–6–4–4 Articulated Engine & Tender' is clearly visible. In actual fact, it *was* a 2–6–2 with tender – Gresley's famous 'V2' class – which emerged from the abandonment of the unusual machine here illustrated.

Below left
In superficial appearance, this Gresley proposed 2–6–4T might be reasonably described as a precursor of the Thompson 'L1' which emerged from the Doncaster Drawing Office some eighteen years after the originating date of this drawing, dated June 1927. There were, however, numerous significant differences, in boiler pressure, driving wheel diameter, tractive effort – in fact, the word 'superficial' is probably right. Gresley's intention, had this engine proceeded beyond the drawing-board, was a locomotive specifically intended for use on the suburban services of the LNER's Great Northern section.

Above right
If Maunsell's first 2–6–4T went out with a bang, then Thompson's 'L1' went out with a whimper, as described on page 112. Designated by BR as Power Classification 4, they never earned the reputation of the Stanier, Fairburn or Riddles engines, also thus classified. As one of Thompson's proposed ten standard types, the 'L1' was designated as a 'mixed-traffic tank'. Thompson retired in June 1946, so most of the class were constructed thereafter.

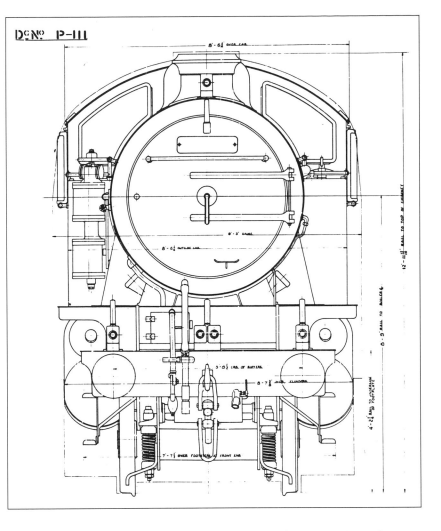

indeed was not an exciting locomotive. Perhaps its epitaph is an appropriate comment on the place in British locomotive annals, of the 2–6–4T wheel arrangement.

Let me end as I began this chapter: by searching for a suitable adjective with which to describe these locomotives. To find one word simultaneously to encapsulate the characteristics of the Great Central's '1B', Maunsell's 'Rivers' and the Fowler tank would be well-nigh impossible. That ten of the BR Standard tanks have been preserved has more to do with their actual survival into 1967 than with their undoubted qualities. Yet even in preservation, rarely will be heard the cry 'Let's go to see the 2–6–4 tank'. Indeed, when *Railway Observer* in February 1963 added that melancholy 'Class extinct' label to the list of 'L1's withdrawn in December 1962, with the familiar sign – 67800† (40E) – I searched in vain anticipation for an epitaph to accompany the passing of the class. There was nothing. In *RO*,

April 1963, there appeared a section headed 'Notes on With-drawals'. The copy read as follows: 'The close of 1962 saw two notable casualties, 'K3' and 'J39', among notable classes that had been a familiar part of the LNER scene for many years.' Details of the life of the 'K3's and 'J39's follow; then comes a mention of Class 'A1/1'. Finally, at the end of the whole section, comes almost as an afterthought a mention of the 'L1's. 'Another large LNER class to vanish at the end of 1962 was Thompson's 5ft 2in "L1" Class 2–6–4T.' There are a few prosaic lines in one paragraph. That was all.

Say 'Thompson' and you think 'B1'. Say 'Stanier' and you think, what? 'Jubilee', 'Black 5', 'Coronation'? Say 'Maunsell' and it's perhaps 'Schools'. Say 'Fowler' and it's 'Royal Scot'. Say 'Riddles' and it's 'Britannia'. Yet of all my many memories of steam, the photograph reproduced on pages 104–5 of this book stands happily in my memory. It was Sunday 14 November 1965. It was a lovely autumn mid-afternoon, at Birkenhead. There was the distant sound of a regular, reliable, rhythmic beat. I was standing – trespassing no doubt – alongside the former Great Western/London and North Western main line, from Birkenhead Woodside to Chester. Coming rapidly, surefootedly and con-fidently up the 1 in 77 grade, Stanier 2–6–4T No. 42606 swept past, with the 14.55 train for Chester and – eventually – Paddington. (Yes, Paddington, where it would arrive, if on time, at 21.10.) No drama, no fuss, no interest: except the click of my faithful Voigtlander. The engine has gone: so has the line at this point. There are no trains, now, from Birkenhead to Paddington. But the memory remains, for ever.

2–6–4 Tank Engines

Class	Railway	Designer	Date Introduced	Number Built
1B	GCR	Robinson	1914	20
K	SECR	Maunsell	1917	20
K1	SECR	Maunsell	1925	1
K	Metropolitan	Hally	1925	6
W	SR	Maunsell	1931	15
4	LMS	Fowler	1927	125
4 (3 cylinder)	LMS	Stanier	1934	37
4 (2 cylinder)	LMS	Stanier	1935	206
4	LMS	Fairburn	1945	277
4MT	BR	Riddles & Jarvis	1951	155
L1	LNER	Thompson	1945	100

7 County Palatine

păl'atine, a & n. 1. (*Count*) *P~*, count having within the territory jurisdiction such as elsewhere belongs only to sovereign (in Eng. Hist. also *Earl P~*); *County P~*, his territory (still in England of Lancashire and Cheshire).

To find an appropriate chapter title for this one, that was simultaneously original and relevant, was not easy. I used both 'Lancashire' and 'Birkenhead' in *In Search of Steam*, and 'North-West Frontier' in *The Call of Steam*. My meanderings around Lancashire, Merseyside and the Wirral needed to be encompassed in some legitimate title that would enable me to write about, and around, the appropriate photographs. As steam retreated, it was in the County Palatine that it was the last to succumb; and it was here that my business and political footsteps led me. To pretend that this was a coincidence would be to deny my own words, to deceive you, and to leave me open to allegations of truancy of which I should properly be found guilty.

My first colour steam photograph in the County Palatine was taken at the erstwhile Manchester Central Station, in March 1963. The next was near the same place, on 31 March 1964. That was an April Fool's Day which I 'celebrated' a day early. It started on a wall, near Stockport. The memory of it remains strong, and the ankle which suffered from it has remained weak to this day. By combining ignorance with bravado and stupidity, I photographed LMS 'Royal Scot' 4–6–0 No. 46129 *The Scottish Horse* bursting under a bridge. My excitement was so great at my 'achievement' that I jumped off the wall onto which I had clambered, in my dark grey business suit, and landed on a lump of rock hidden in the grass. It was about 6 p.m. and my destination was the Midland Hotel, Manchester. Instead, I made for the nearest hospital, driving in great pain as my ankle swelled visibly by the minute. That my ankle was not broken was more

by luck than by good judgement. The photograph, late in the day at the end of winter, was artistically poor, not least because the train appeared unexpectedly as I reached the top of the wall. It was on the move, and fast colour film for everyday use had not been invented.

The writing of these words prompts me to study the map that was my guide that day, and which is beside me now: Ordnance Survey, Sheet 101, Manchester. In those days, OS maps had on their covers the date on which each map was fully revised, and published; in this case 1958–59 and 1961 respectively. Where precisely was I? Was it actually Stockport? From the mists of time emerges the name 'New Mills', rather than Stockport. Also from that sub-conscious depth comes a still, small voice that tells me it was a Manchester to Buxton businessman's express. Hauled by a 'Scot'? I do not know. Shall I guess or try to work it out by reference to the relevant timetables? My hoarding instinct never lets me throw away a timetable from my steam-photography years. Shall we try to discover where I was, and what train it was that, fortunately, lives in my collection? Let's take out my well-worn copy of British Railways' Passenger Services Timetable, London to the Midlands, North Wales and the North, for 9 September 1963 to 14 June 1964.

The lengthy saga of this poor photograph is recounted on page 113. The precise location still eludes me, but Dick Hargreave, Director of Development and Town Planning for Stockport, has said that he will 'research' it, on this book's publication. It was 31 March 1964: the train was the 5.30 p.m. Manchester Central to Buxton and the engine was 'Royal Scot' 4–6–0 No. 46129 *The Scottish Horse*, in a quite deplorable condition.

Where precisely was I? Research for this chapter indicates New Mills as a more likely location than the Stockport area. The first person providing correct identification, duly corroborated to Dick Hargreave's satisfaction, will be sent a memento of some sort, by me!

Where do we start? *Table 97*: Manchester to Buxton and Crewe. Stockport Edgeley. New Mills Newtown. Or *Table 182*: Manchester and Buxton to Derby, Stockport Tiviot Dale, New Mills Central? Surely not *Table 185*: Manchester to Stockport, Marple, Macclesfield and Hayfield? As I peruse the yellowing pages of a timetable which is, I suppose, almost an historic document – yet it is only 20 years old – I curse my ignorance, my failure to appreciate the passing of history that was within my grasp, yet contemporaneously beyond my boundaries of interest and knowledge. Look at that timetable. 'Railhead Distribution Scheme' says the advertisement on page 351, below Table 97. 'Liquids in Bulk' – page 354. Turn to table 182. More 'Liquids in Bulk' – on page 510. What *was* that train? The 5.30 p.m. (no 17.30, yet) Manchester Central/Cheadle Heath/Chinley/Chapel-en-le-Frith/Peak Forest/Millers Dale/Buxton? Maybe it was earlier than my memory recalls: perhaps the 4.45 p.m. Manchester Piccadilly/Stockport Edgeley/Disley/New Mills Newtown/Whaley Bridge/Chapel-en-le-Frith South/Buxton? The late Selwyn Lloyd's words about me, at an election meeting in Birkenhead in 1966, flash through my mind – 'splendid chap, Robert Adley: relies on his memory for his jokes and his imagination for his facts!!' Thank you, sir. In truth, I cannot tell from the timetable.

How about the map? Was I driving to Manchester on the A6? Naturally, New Mills is right on the edge of that map: it would be. Something tells me that the bridge in question is just off the A6, perhaps by New Mills Newtown Station. It *was* New Mills, rather than Stockport, I think . . .

What about *The Scottish Horse*? Perhaps Peter Hands and 'What Happened to Steam' will give me a clue. According to him, 46129 was shedded at Manchester Longsight in March 1963. Well, that seems good intelligence, even likelihood but still I do not *know*. Maybe some kind reader will tell me what my memory cannot recall. Meantime, such rambling, inconsequential reminiscence tells its own tale. Perhaps one final search for information would help to solve my inability accurately to identify the train or its location. '*Railway Observer* is perhaps worth a glance', I soliloquise as I write. 31 March 1964: probably the June edition might conceivably provide a clue. So, without much more than a fleeting hope, I turn to the section headed 'London Midland Region', and run my eye down the area subheadings. 'Ashchurch: Nottingham: Rowsley'. That's not too far. 'As from Monday 27 April, Rowsley goods yard was closed to all traffic. The shed is to be retained as a stabling point for banking locomotives, but most of its allocation has been transferred away.' There follows the familiar list of locomotives.

'Nothing there for me'. I muse. 'What's next?' Manchester.

The first paragraph under this heading described diesel training of drivers that was taking place between Manchester Central and Wigan. Ugh! I read the next few words – and gulped with disbelief:

The 5.30 p.m. from Manchester Central (SX) and 8.0 a.m. from Buxton are regularly worked by Royal Scot 4–6–0s. 46129(9A) – minus name plates and in a deplorable external condition – seems to be the regular engine, relieved at times by 46140.

I read and re-read the piece four or five times. There we are then; more than 20 years after the photograph was taken, I now know which train it was and that it was not Stockport. Was it New Mills? Map reference 998850 looks a likely spot, just off the A6. Perhaps, if I include the shot in the book, albeit a poor one, someone may recognise the exact location.

This chapter is entitled 'County Palatine' and that lengthy preamble about 46129 took place at the far south-eastern corner of the area thus designated by the Concise Oxford Dictionary and quoted on page 113. The use of Manchester as a commercial centre for my activities as Sales Director of the May Fair Hotel became more regular. Having crippled myself jumping off that wall, I had to leave the car in Manchester and return to London the following day, 1 April, by train, (12.25 Manchester Central to St Pancras): not that that was a hardship, but Jane was none too polite.

By 22 April I was back in Manchester, and on the trail of steam. I 'discovered' Clifton Junction: thereafter the County Palatine became my Mecca: no other word will do. Although imbued with a strong affection for the Manchester area, and latterly for Merseyside, it would be foolish to pretend that I possessed an intimate knowledge of the railway geography of the area. However, ignorance is not only bliss, it often provided one, in hindsight, with opportunities that deception could subsequently claim as wisdom. In other words – because I did not really know where to go, I went to the nearest place concomitant with the interests of my employer and my first constituency. Consequently, from the viewpoint of railway photography, many unfashionable, possibly unattractive and often unusual places, came within the aim of my camera, such as that bridge, from under which *The Scottish Horse* erupted.

My main areas of camerawork in the 'Counties Palatine' were Manchester itself; Birkenhead; and latterly around Lostock Hall and Rose Grove. Notwithstanding the industrial nature of these locations, both Lancashire and Cheshire abound in beautiful

There was a lusty, rhinoceros-like atmosphere surrounding the 'Miles Platting Charge' which heralded the approach to the Bank through Manchester Victoria Station. Steam-hauled trains not taking a banker – one or two of which were always standing ready on 'Wall-Side Pilot' duty in the station – made a vigorous assault, and regularly produced a monumental and magnificent display. For many years, Aspinall L & Y 0–6–0s performed the banking task, but 'Black 5s' were there in the final days. Camera problems, infuriatingly, made unusable many of my shots of this dramatic event in the closing months of steam, as is self-evident from this particular effort. I can only hope that you share my view that a bad photograph is better than none.

Less than twelve months now until the end of steam in the County Palatine, and in Britain: it is 10 August 1967 as BR Standard '5' 4–6–0 No. 73158 blasts through Manchester Victoria with an empty stock train: she has only a few weeks active service left.

Note the dreaded d.m.u. at the platform on the left.

countryside. Indeed, much of it is off the tourist track, some distance from the mountain and lakeland scenery in the north. Those 'unfashionable, possibly unattractive and often unusual places' that I visited were but a handful of locations at which steam was still well in evidence in Spring 1964, the date at which my visits to the area began to become fairly regular. I have mentioned Clifton Junction; another spot full of nostalgic memories is Warrington. Dallam Shed (8B) was seemingly somewhat neglected by enthusiasts, as I never recall seeing another photographer, or even number-taker there. The shed was adjacent to the west side of the main (LNWR) line, about a mile north of Bank Quay Station. Thus, a shed visit gave one ample opportunity to get alongside the main line. Perhaps it was because it was about half-an-hour's walk from the station that it attracted few visitors, although my time there was during mid-week truancy. I know not what it was like at weekends.

Conversely, my numerous visits to Birkenhead Shed were almost always at weekends, the first of which was on 11 July 1965 following my adoption as Prospective Conservative Parliamentary Candidate for the Birkenhead constituency. Contrary to popular myth, candidates receive no remuneration for their travelling or any other expenses. I was lucky in that the contemporary chairman of the Oxton Conservative Club, Don MacIntyre, worked in Harrow and lived in Birkenhead, so he gave me a lift up on Friday afternoons most weekends. Jane and our infant son, Simon, mostly stayed at home in Sunningdale whilst I undertook my speaking, canvassing and other political activities. Don and I would return south in the early hours – about 4.30 a.m. – on the Monday mornings so I had Sunday to myself in and around Birkenhead. Much of this time was spent at Birkenhead Shed, with which I became very familiar. The railway staff were somewhat taken aback at first by the presence of the Conservative candidate in their midst. In those days – it's only 20 years ago, but seems a lifetime – there was still an old-fashioned image of the political parties which was totally alien to me. My shed visits had no hidden politcal purpose, however, and I was accepted for what I was – a railway enthusiast.

It is my ambition and intent never to impart political indoctrination or content into my books, and fortunately railway enthusiasm is a completely classless occupation. My ample time at Birkenhead (8H) enabled me thoroughly to explore the shed. Its access on to the main line was via a steep incline out of the shed, which on damp, frosty mornings produced splendidly photogenic slipping and spinning wheels. I saw all the seasons there, from ice, fog, frost and damp, to hot, still stifling days in July and August, when, with many engines on shed at the weekend, a thick choking soupy haze enveloped the area. The exit road was actually on to a short spur on the west side of the Chester line about three-quarters of a mile south of Birkenhead Woodside Station: from here one looked across to the carriage sidings, and away across the Mersey to Liverpool's familiar cathedral-dominated skyline.

Let us, as the gazetteers would say, now take ourselves off to Liverpool. The city, although in Lancashire, has always exuded a totally different character from the rest of the county of which it geographically forms part. Few cities arouse such passions as this place, granted its Charter by King John in 1207. The growth of the port of Liverpool paralleled the growth in trade with America. Between 1715 when the first commercial dock in Britain was created, and 1847 when the first floating landing stage was opened, 16 docks were completed, with famous names like Canning, Albert, Trafalgar, Brunswick. Brunswick Dock was the site of the early terminus, replaced in 1874 by Central Station with its splendid arched roof. Development continued north and south of Pier Head, with 8 miles of docks and nearly 40 miles of quayside, threaded from end to end with railway lines, and a kaleidoscope of locomotives. From 1893 to 1956, the Liverpool Overhead Railway, the first overhead electric railway in the world, ran for $6\frac{1}{4}$ miles along the waterfront. Notwithstanding the fact that it carried ten million passengers a year, it was closed for want of £2 million investment to renew the decking. Lest it be thought that this is a frustrated gazetteer's guide to Liverpool, it has to be said that both the docks, the railway and steam were in rapid retreat by 4 July 1965, the date of my first railway photography in Liverpool itself, at Bank Hall Shed (8K), situated on the west side of the line between Sandhills and Kirkdale Stations. Bank Hall Shed was the main Lancashire and Yorkshire Railway (L & Y) depot in Liverpool, and in its day housed the main L & Y passenger engines, although until about 1920 it was known as Sandhills rather than Bank Hall, and the signal box by the shed's rail entrance was designated 'Sandhills No. 2'.

Bank Hall, designated 8K in the major reorganisation of September 1963, was for years home for the famous and delightful L & Y 'Pugs' which were for long a familiar sight in the nearby docks. Sadly they had gone – the last being withdrawn in October 1961 – by the time I paid my first and only visit. There were two 'Jubilees' on shed: No. 45684 *Jutland* was simmering inside the shed (see *Call of Steam* page 41), whilst No. 45721 *Impregnable* had already lost its nameplate, either the target of souvenir hunters or removed by BR before it could be stolen. Bank Hall 'Jubilees' were still entrusted with important duties, 45721 working the 14.00 Glasgow-Liverpool train on 2/3 July

1965. There were 'Black 5's, BR Standard '4' and '5' 4–6–0s and an Ivatt 'Flying Pig' on shed which I managed to photograph.

By this date, the only other steam sheds left in the city were Aintree – another L & Y stronghold – Edge Hill and Speke Junction, both the latter two being LNWR establishments. Having 'done' Bank Hall on 4 July, I visited Edge Hill the following weekend. Although one engine seen and photographed was LMS '3F' 0–6–0T No. 47406, not until I came to write these words and check the fate of some of the engines that ended their BR days in the County Palatine, did I realise that 47406 has subsequently been in front of my lens in another incarnation – at Barry, whence she has now escaped to the Peak Railway.

From Edge Hill shed, it was but a simple trespass to the carriage sidings. By July 1965 the overhead electrification works north-wards from Crewe were already part of the landscape, and the sight of a 'Jinty' under the wires was not only incongruous, but also painful in ramming home the realisation that the days of steam were well and truly numbered. The sight of sand being shovelled in front of the slipping wheels, on greasy rails; of the game little tank struggling with a lengthy rake of empty stock, will always be with me. As a photographic location, the main line at Edge Hill is immortalised by the stunning artistry of the late Bishop Eric Treacy.

My Birkenhead visits continued through 1965, and amongst my fortunate sights was GWR 'Modified Hall' 4–6–0 No. 7924, *Thornycroft Hall* on 11 July. By this date it was easy to have forgotten the Great Western's once-substantial presence in Birkenhead, where GWR and LMS stood shoulder-to-shoulder. Indeed, as I photographed Stanier 2–6–4T No. 42606 pounding up from Woodside on the (Sunday) 14.55 train from Birkenhead to Chester and Paddington (see pages 104–5) it was with – yet again – regret that I bemoaned that fate had not brought me here years earlier, to watch GWR 4–6–0s heading the through trains to London from their northern outpost. The last GWR engines were moved away from Birkenhead shed in 1963. Woodside Station itself closed on 6 November 1967, when Rock Ferry became the terminal for passenger trains from the Chester direction.

Only those either with poor memories or no knowledge of railway history will be surprised to recall the fact that the LNER managed an appearance – and thus rates a fleeting mention in this chapter – in the Palatinate. The Cheshire Lines Committee (CLC) main line ran from Manchester to Liverpool, and up to Southport, and the Great Central, together with the Great Northern and Midland Railways, eventually owned the CLC, whose head-quarters were at Liverpool Central Station. With the grouping of

As if the incongruity of an ancient-looking tank-engine under the electrified wires is not itself a poignant reminder of the change from living steam to lifeless electric traction, the disembarking railwayman is about to shovel sand, recalling the struggle of man against the elements. Wet rails, slipping wheels, a heavy rake of empty stock: a struggle indeed for LMS '3F' 0–6–0T No. 47519 at Edge Hill Carriage Sidings, on 11 July 1965.

The railway scene in Liverpool is unrecogniseable today, from that date just over twenty years ago: it seems a lifetime. 47519, for years an Edge Hill (8A) engine, was withdrawn some four months after this scene was recorded. Edge Hill was home to some of the most famous and powerful locomotives in the land. Was the decline of Liverpool synonymous with the end of steam? And does the cheerful spirit of Bishop Eric Treacy not still live on, hereabouts?

1923, the Great Central became part of the LNER, although the
CLC remained the premier joint railway in Britain, and indeed the
only one to retain its own management down to 1947. The CLC as
its name implies, had a significant presence in Cheshire through
its other main line to Chester: whilst the Great Central's line from
Chester ran up through the centre of the Wirral peninsular, to
Bidston where it joined the Wirral Railway. Railway history
hereabouts is fascinating but complex and rewards detailed
study. Bidston itself remains a junction and indeed the terminating point for the second-class-only service to Wrexham, which
owes its existence more to railway history than to modern traffic-
pattern design. The service on this line does not exactly 'connect'
with the other trains through Bidston, on the West Kirby to
Liverpool Central electric service.

When I visited Bidston on 30 October 1965, the John Summers
Iron Ore trains were still '9F'-hauled, and a 'Jinty' was fussing
around the station-yard. The following day I paid a late afternoon
visit to Speke Junction Shed (8C) which had an air of depression
and decay about it, although it somehow hung on as a steam shed
until 6 May 1968, one of the last survivors. Compared to the other
Liverpool sheds, it seemed always to have been unexciting. What
would one have given to have been able to photograph some of
Merseyside's earlier railway history?

Bidston, on the Wirral Peninsula, seems to have escaped the attention of railway photographers. Doubtless its flat terrain, lack of major railway installations yet proximity to so many so much more interesting locations, accounts therefor, although with two triangular layouts Bidston a century ago would have provided ample variety of train movements. The station was in an isolated position as recently as 30 October 1965, when I took this shot nearby, of '9F' 2–10–0 No. 92047 with steam to spare on a train of empty John Summers iron-ore wagons. I have not been back since.

Although these heavy John Summers trains were well-known as a '9F' duty, they too seem to have attracted less attention than the more photogenic Tyne Dock-Consett, or the Long Meg-Widnes anhydrite trains with their fierce gradients and scenic grandeur respectively.

Note the electrified third rail.

My Manchester visits enabled me to see most of the sheds in and around the city that saw out the steam era. Between business appointments I would try to grab the odd half-hour beside a line where steam might appear. Once, in Oldham, I found myself in a snowstorm clambering through a fence at the end of a small cul-de-sac, where I photographed an unidentified Ivatt or BR Standard '2' 2–6–0 shunting in a weird, enclosed, walled place that I have never subsequently been able to locate. Even the date eludes me, save that it was in a roll of film, the first and last exposures of which were made on 10 December 1965 and 20 March 1966, and its immediate 'neighbours' were shots at Birkenhead on 9 January and Mold Junction on 20 March. It certainly looks the epitome of a photograph taken in Oldham.

The conclusion of the General Election campaign of 1966 ended my reasons, excuses, opportunities – call it what you will – regularly to visit Birkenhead, where I took my last photographs at the shed on 7 May that year. During the election campaign I managed to get to Chester shed on the Sunday before polling day, with some undistinguished photographs to show for my trouble.

As 1967 dawned, steam's eclipse was clearly only a matter of time. Although my business life was so arranged as to enable me to continue visits to the North-West, my weekends were concentrated in the Bristol area, since my adoption as Prospective Candidate in that city where lived Jane's family. My records recall a further visit to Speke Junction Shed on 26 July 1967, when only 'Black 5's and '8F's were to be seen. I was to snatch the odd moments on Manchester Victoria or Exchange station, as well as a shot of 'Black 5' No. 45454 at Liverpool Lime Street on 25 July. Then in August came the first of many visits to Lostock Hall Shed, near Preston, destined to be one of the three survivors to the final, bitter end of steam. To catalogue each and every visit to Lancashire in that final year would achieve little, especially as I was having problems with my camera. It became a time of great melancholia, as once-busy steam sheds closed, stations and lines likewise.

On 4 June 1968, I took some shots at Haslingden, on the erstwhile L & Y Accrington to Stubbins line; abandoned when the line closed on 7 November 1960. By now, it was a matter of weeks to the end. For reasons I cannot recall, I took no photographs during the first five months of 1968, but on that 4 June it is clear from my records that little or no work was done for my employers. Amongst my locations, including Haslingden, was the Farington curve; Lostock Hall Station, Shed and Junction; Mintholme; Rose Grove Shed and Station: and Burnley Central, where the mills which feature in every photograph are themselves sadly an anachronistic reminiscence.

Whilst Lostock Hall and Rose Grove seduced me throughout June and July 1968, I managed a visit to the third of the last surviving sheds, Carnforth, on 25 June. That we can still photograph Carnforth's concrete coaling-tower, its base often sheathed in steam, is a blessed reminder of days spent on shed in Lancashire. I got through rolls of film that day, which I finished at Bolton. Again I kicked myself as, standing at the north end of Trinity Street Station, the crossovers and gradient on the triangle represented yet another opportunity missed. The following day came my last visit to Speke Junction – and, before one knew it, it was 31 July.

To my dying day I shall remember the feeling of that last week of steam. Misery is to be endured alone, not suffered as a corporate emotion. Having no wish to be amongst my fellows at this depressing hour, it was still possible to escape and to capture steam in one's lens in solitude. There was nobody else at Rose Grove West Junction to observe the last days of steam haulage down to Padiham Power Station; or at Mintholme Crossing, grid reference 599262 on Ordnance Survey Map No. 94. Here, quite alone, in pleasant, open country, industrial Lancashire seemed far away. As '8F' 2–8–0s trundled by, it was easy to forget that we should never see such mundane scenes again . . . ever. Briefly, a plan was mooted to put some '8F's into mothballs as a strategic reserve in case of a fuel crisis or national emergency. It came to naught.

No. 48340, in an utterly filthy state, was the last locomotive I saw and photographed, that awful day. By now I was at Cherry Tree Junction, on the edge of Blackburn, as she plodded by on an eastbound freight from the Preston direction. For some years a Northwich engine 48340, like an unloved orphan, gawky, dirty, and uncared-for, was shoved from place to place: to Birkenhead in February 1965: to Aintree two months later: back to Northwich in June '67; to Rose Grove the following March: the next month to Bolton; then finally back to Rose Grove. Ultimately she, like her few remaining sisters, featured in the final roll-call of '8F's to survive until the very bitter end of steam. Transferred to Lostock Hall shed after withdrawal, she was reported in *Railway Observer* still to be there on 27 September. During November, 48340 made her final journey; unloved, unsung, unnoticed and not destined for preservation she was towed away towards Beighton, Sheffield, and cut up there in December; in the cold mid-winter, long long ago . . .

Previous page
It is snowing. Somewhere in Oldham, in the early weeks of 1966. The light is unfit for colour photography, let alone of moving trains. Unusually, my records are imprecise. Oldham: the very name is synonymous with industrial Lancashire. The names of the stations have – or had – a Victorian ring: Glodwick Road; Mumps; Clegg Street; and Central, of course. Geography dictated tunnels and steep gradients – the early route to Oldham from Manchester Victoria being via Middleton Junction and the rope-worked 1 in 27 Werneth Incline – but this is merely a caption, not a place for recounting railway history, although the tale of the erstwhile Stationmaster at Mumps, one Thomas Normington, is in keeping with the character of this part of the County Palatine. He it was who recalled the problems, in 1848, when Oldham to Blackpool day tickets were sold at 1s. 6d. for gentlemen and 1s. 0d. for ladies, resulting in an early case of the use of 'drag' for financial advantage.

Here, an unidentified Ivatt or BR Standard '2' 2–6–0 shunts an Oldham siding, the identity of which perhaps someone may recognise and advise me. My only photograph anywhere in Oldham. Dark Satanic mills abound . . .

8 Legacy of Churchward

In my view, albeit both unprofessional and prejudiced, George Jackson Churchward was the supreme steam railway mechanical engineer. In terms of design advances, he was a giant; in terms of locomotive appearance, he was an artist. A pupil on the South Devon Railway and then on the Great Western at Swindon, he became Works Manager there in 1896 and followed William Dean as Locomotive, Carriage and Wagon Superintendent in 1902. Chief Mechanical Engineer 1916–21, he was the greatest locomotive engineer of his time. It is not too much to claim that his work on the GWR put that railway into a pre-eminent position which it retained certainly during the 20 years of his reign at Swindon; arguably until the mid-thirties; some would say until the end of steam on British Rail. The pride he instilled into all ends of the GWR empire, permeated throughout the railway; and that pride, devolved into an understandable spirit of superiority, survives to this day on parts of Western Region.

The story of Churchward's life, and indeed the irony and tragedy of his death, have been told many times, and it is not my intention to reiterate it here. Indeed, his mechanical achievements are exceedingly well documented, and my ignorance of things mechanical disqualifies me from repeating, let alone embellishing, his profound impact on locomotive practice and performance. I have just two points to make: firstly, the appearance of his locomotives was quite outstanding and they stood the test of time; secondly, his hallmark, perpetuated by his successors Collett and Hawksworth, stamped his hand indelibly on their locomotives, that clearly bear his imprint. You will expect me to seek to justify these assertions, so let me try.

Before attempting my justification, it is necessary to repeat my oft-made confession of ignorance of matters technical. Of course, I could copy or plagiarise the words of others on the technical similarities, about numbers of cylinders, long-travel valves and such visibly obvious features as wheel arrangements. However,

my respect for readers of my books includes the assumption that my ignorance is readily obvious; as well as the recognition that detailed technical information is readily available in numerous sophisticated tomes dedicated to the subject of the mechanical engineering *minutiae* of the steam-engine. Discarding the verbal diarrhoea which is the hallmark of my books, it really all boils down, as between Churchward, Collett and Hawksworth to a clearly visible family likeness; and that is more or less as far as I intend to go, in a chapter dedicated to the father of 20-century GWR locomotive design and practice. If 'every picture tells a story', then outward appearances tell their own tale.

Knowledgeable readers will by now have begun to wonder why the name 'Stanier' has yet to appear in this chapter. Indeed, Brian Haresnape sought to persuade me to insert it between 'Collett' and 'Hawksworth' throughout. That I decided not so to do has nothing to do with an attempt to deny the clear link: indeed Stanier himself, were he editing this chapter, would doubtless have insisted that his debt to Churchward be formally recognised. My reason is simply that this chapter is intended to be *about* the GWR, for which I make no apology. The 'Princess Royal' was a 'King' with Pacific frame layout; and Stanier's first 2–6–0 even had a GWR safety valve casing on the domeless

Hardly the masterpiece by which George Jackson Churchward is remembered, but nevertheless longlived albeit small – both in size and number – was the '1361' Class 0–6–0ST. In fact they were a non-standard design built with as much Churchward current practice as was practicable. Based on an ancient Cornwall Railway design, the five engines bear the Churchward name, but are also attributable to Holcroft. Introduced in 1910, they were ideal for docksides and wharves with tight curves. They were classified 0F.

Most of the photographs of these engines at work seem to be in and around the docks and at Laira, Plymouth; but by January 1957 they were allocated to Swindon and Taunton. All were withdrawn by the end of boiler, albeit removed at Stanier's insistence when it emerged. This made it clear beyond peradventure that much of his work for the LMS was indeed part of the 'legacy of Churchward'. Nonetheless, may I crave your indulgence by not inserting the name Stanier on my chart on page 132. If I did so, then 'Jubilee', 'Black 5', Rebuilt 'Scot' and 'Patriot', '8F', '2P' and '3P' 2–6–2T, as well as the '5F' 2–6–0 would need to be inserted: not to mention Maunsell's Moguls which surely, too, were clearly part-plagiarised from the great man. Indeed the mere insertion of this paragraph perhaps makes the point well enough, namely that the legacy of Churchward went far beyond the bounds of his own time and far beyond the geographical limits of the Great Western Railway.

Assuming my unsophisticated assertion has not thus far caused apoplexy amongst the *cognoscenti*, perhaps my two points, referred to above, can only really be justified in a very crude manner: 'appearance' and 'imprint' were, if you recall, the two points I offered as evidence. For 'appearance' I can offer a few rather poor photographs; for 'imprint', a list of some of the locomotives designed by Churchward, and for which I assert my claim that his successors' engines, bore his imprint. A crude list may make my point; and of course it is necessary to stress, and stress again, that the GWR did not begin with Churchward, who would today were he alive, and did when he was, acknowledge the immense achievements of his predecessors, from Gooch to Dean. Indeed Churchward himself closely studied and copied American practice: his greatness was his willingness to experiment and to change.

The chart on page 132 is not a comprehensive or detailed guide to all the Churchward, Collett and Hawksworth locomotives. It is intended only to illustrate the continuity of appearance of the three men's locomotives and covers *only* those locomotives some of the members of the 'family' of which I was able to see and photograph during 1962–68, with their antecedence thus indicated. I am indebted to Brian Haresnape's outstanding *Pictorial History* series for much information: amongst the best railway books ever written.

The purpose of this chart is limited solely to justifying my chapter-title, itself perhaps little more than an excuse to include a random selection of GWR photographs: and there seems no need to apologise for that. By the end of 1962, when my photo-mission began, the number of classes of GWR locomotives still on the active list had already dwindled, but notwithstanding withdrawals, it is surely true that, compared to the LMS, LNER, and SR stock extant, there were in fact far fewer different classes in existence, due to the 'family' policy of standardisation based on

boilers, which is the verification of the intellectually-limited point being made by this chapter. Perhaps, in appearance, the only really original locomotive, judged solely on the criterion of external appearance, produced by Collett, was his 22xx class. For

'Family'	Churchward	Collett	Hawksworth
4–6–0	Saint Star	Castle Hall King Grange Manor	Modified Hall County
2–8–0	2800	(2884)	
2–8–0	4700	—	—
2–6–2T	5101 3100 + others 4400	8100 5101/ 6100	
2–8–0T	4200	7200	
2–6–0	4300		
0–6–0PT	(Developed the Pannier concept)	5700	1600

132

The Collett '61xx' Class of 2–6–2T were clearly a direct derivative of the earlier Churchward engines of this wheel-arrangement: and why change a winning team? As the '61xx' were an update of the '5101' class, so the latter were directly related to the Churchward '31xx' Class of 1903.

The '61xx' Class virtually monopolised the GW London area surburban services from their introduction in the early 'thirties to their ousting by the ghastly tin-can d.m.u.'s more than twenty years later. Their qualities were such that other duties were then readily found for them. Of the seventy engines built, between 1931 and 1935, some 55 were still active in the winter of 1962–3: and 31 were still in service at January 1965, the last year of Western Region steam.

Here, on 30 June 1963, No. 6133 is shunting vans in Southall Station: note 'CHESTER' on the London Midland van. She was withdrawn in December that year. How better to remember these fine and handsome locomotives, than to recall their memory as one sees a d.m.u. desecrate Sonning cutting. Ugh!

Hawksworth, even so modest a claim is quite hard to make, save perhaps for his 15xx Pannier, which utilised ideas from the 'USA' 0–6–0T.

In conclusion, let me make clear that it is no part of my purpose, in any way, to criticise Collett and Hawksworth: someone had to follow Churchward, and in my eyes they are increased, not diminished, in stature, by continuing to build on such firm foundations. Collett was an able engineer in his own right, but maintained Churchward's principles and ideas. After all, is Edward Thompson universally eulogised for his attempts to 'exterminate' the Gresley look? Merely to ask the question, is to answer it.

From the day in February 1902 when new 4–6–0 No. 100 emerged from Swindon, to the appearance in 1945 of the final GWR two-cylinder class, the 'Counties', was a time-span that wrought a transformation in the manner, method, and style of transportation. Yet the 'Counties' – numbered 1000–1029 – were clearly recognisable as direct descendants of No. 100, and of the next two 4–6–0s, No. 98 and No. 171, with which Churchward stamped his mark indelibly on Swindon. (Although Churchward did not officially take over from Dean as Locomotive, Carriage and Wagon Superintendent until 1902, he had been Works Manager at Swindon since 1896, and there can be no doubt that No. 100 was Churchward's inspiration.) His determination to standardise the locomotive fleet, and his success in so doing was naturally perpetuated through the 1923 grouping. Thus, of the 'Big Four' railways, the GWR alone was able, naturally, easily and uninterruptedly to continue with its style and practice.

Railway history thus favoured engineering continuity. The legacy of Churchward was ensured. Indeed, as already mentioned, his influence spread far beyond his GWR. On the Southern Railway, Maunsell took note of Churchward's practice, as did Gresley, reluctantly, on the LNER. Stanier, of course, was a Swindon man; whilst Ivatt and Riddles both held key positions in the Stanier LMS administration. The 'BR Standard' developments owed more than a nod to the great man. The influence of his principles was felt throughout our railway system. But it was the GWR that was his lasting monument – and a great legacy indeed.

Churchward was the father of the modern Great Western, its locomotives and its pride. There was an indefinable superiority not only about 'things' Great Western, but about people Great Western too. Thus, if someone were to ask you, on a wet Sunday two days before Christmas, to travel by public transport over 100 miles, and to finish up on top of a bus, listening to the conversation of a dozen old men, it is possible that the appeal of such an event might be hard to discern. If, however, the

destination was Bristol Temple Meads Station; the occasion was the triumphant return of 'King' 4–6–0 No. 6023 *King Edward II*; and the men on the bus an assemblage of former GWR enginemen come together to join in the triumphant celebrations, then railway enthusiasts will understand the force that dragged me from the bosom of my family, the wrapping paper and the tinsel, on 23 December 1984.

'Pat Lewis fired to ''Gentleman'' Bert Davis, on the 4.25 to Salop.' 'Bill Donnington fired to Bill ''Spinnaker'' Hawkins.' 'Bill used to burn 2 ton more coal than I did.' 'John Wood was firing to Jimmy Russe on the Ghost Train; and on the two ''Kings'' coupled, light-engine, through the Severn Tunnel on route-proving turns.' 'Ronald Gardner, who in his time fired and drove from both Bristol's GWR sheds, Bath Road and St Philips Marsh, was the local representative for the GWR's Enginemen and Firemen's Mutual Assurance Society.'

To listen to these men swapping banter and reminiscences was to be a privileged guest at the table of the railway aristocracy. There was no more dignified calling than to be a senior engine driver on the Great Western Railway. John Wood, who joined the GWR in 1930, told me about his footplate work on the two 'Kings'. Towards the end of the war – he thought it was 1944 – it

Britain's first 2–8–0's were Churchward's '28xx' Class. Introduced in 1903, they were so reliable, sturdy and satisfactory that, with minor modifications, Collett had more built between 1938 and 1942. The end indeed was nigh, for Great Western steam, by 15 March 1965 – in less than a year, this sight at Bristol Temple Meads would be but a memory, as one of the Collett engines, No. 3855, drags a heavy eastbound freight through the station. It was based at Croes Newydd at this time and faces a long journey home. Having languished at Barry since withdrawal, this engine still holds tenuously to the prospect of life through its purchase by Mr G Rippingale.

134

No. 6028 *King George VI* languishes, dead, forlorn, discarded and bereft of name and number plates at Old Oak Common on 23 June 1963, some six months after withdrawal. Quite simply, the 'Kings' were the most powerful 4–6–0's in Britain – and they knew it. Really the ultimate development of Churchward's 'Stars', they could and would surely have lasted for ever had man so decreed.

Dare I say it – the sight of 6028 here at Old Oak is more evocative than the vision of a preserved engine, pristine, gleaming and unreal, that is welcome but commonplace today. That *was* the end of the steam era: this is how we remember them. . . . .

was decided to check on the suitability of the 'Kings' on the Cardiff road, where they hadn't run before. 'Being the GWR naturally we didn't just try one engine, but two coupled together. When the Great Western carried out a test on anything, it made sure . . .' He went on to tell me of his subsequent runs on the 4.25 p.m. Bristol Temple Meads to Shrewsbury train, which ran through the Severn Tunnel, turned north at Maindee Junction, Newport, and was first stop Pontypool Road.

This must have been an interesting train, of which I knew nothing prior to listening to Pat Lewis. From John Wood came details of the 'Ghost Train', and his confident assertions of regular 90-minute non-stop runs, with a 'King' and six coaches, from Temple Meads to Paddington. Bill Donnington, Reg Gazzard and others confirmed the validity of a very special war-time train. As told to me – doubtless this has been well documented, although I have never heard or read of it – the 'Ghost Train' comprised six coaches held in a siding by Dr Day's Junction, Bristol. This was at a time when the Luftwaffe were attacking the airfields of south-eastern England. According to John, Whitchurch Airfield was out of range of these attacks, and was thus much used by the most important military and political leaders, who would be flown in, whisked to Temple Meads, and hastened

at top speed to Paddington. A 'King' from Bath Road shed would be alerted, the stock brought from Dr Day's into Temple Meads, the engine attached, the road cleared, and all traffic removed from the path for the VIP's high-speed run to London. John Wood himself recalls firing on the 'Ghost Train' on a number of occasions and numbered amongst his passengers Churchill, Eisenhower, and 'Vinegar Joe' Stillwell. 'They've just about matched the Ghost Train's times now, with those so-called High Speed Trains.'

If Ghosts rest easy only in the knowledge that they and their works are appreciated and immortalised, then George Jackson Churchward rests eternally at ease: and deserves so to do. I salute him.

The Churchward Masterpiece – the freight personification of *The Great Bear*: 47xx 2–8–0 No. 4700, withdrawn and awaiting her fate, at Bristol St Philip's Marsh on 26 January 1963. She appeared in 1919 with a No. 1 boiler with specially lengthened smokebox. Fact, of course, disproves fantasy that it was *The Great Bear* rebuilt, as the Pacific was not withdrawn for conversion until 1924! However, it was the use of No. 111 on the Cocoa Trains that germinated the seeds of the potential for No. 4700: thus my imaginative opening to this caption, to which purists will object, but romantics may accede.

9 Out of Town

Not for the first time and not for the last, I have already written too much and Blandford Press are urging restraint on my 'word factory'. There is no room for my notional chapters on 'Third Rail Steam' or 'Jinty Parade'. But a series of articles written for the magazine bearing the title at the top of this page enables me to include a chapter more photographic than verbal. My thesis is simple.

There is more to railways than steam engines. Indeed, what was once simply described as the 'magic of the railway' is today formalised, dignified and packaged as industrial archaeology. Nevertheless, 'the railway' fills a unique place in our hearts and minds, associated as it ever will be with the opening-up of our

Jane + 2! For the smallest county in England, Rutland has a rich and varied railway history, which cannot be encompassed in a caption. Post-Beeching 'rationalisation' – that awful euphemism for mass closure – has decimated the once-numerous east–west routes across the Midlands and, perhaps surprisingly, the former Midland Railway route into Peterborough, through Oakham, is the survivor.

Going 'Out of Town' however need not only encompass visits to closed and lifted lines. Often, rural footpaths cross railway lines in places mercifully inaccessible to the motor car. Just such an agreeable Rutland location can be enjoyed on a footpath from Wing, which crosses the Manton to Luffenham line at map reference 897035 on OS Sheet 141 in the 1:50000 series. Jane, Tom and George pose here, just by the River Chater – England still almost unspoiled.

nation and of its people to our countryside. The railway created towns with its arrival; and broke them with its departure. To eulogise the architectural heritage of Britain's railways is not my aim in this brief chapter. Be it Ribblehead Viaduct, Box Tunnel or the great arch of St Pancras Station, the signature of the system is clear, as characterised by these great national monuments. But some there be, which have no memorial. Their track-beds are overgrown, their bridges and culverts, ere long-lived, now rest in peace.

Across Britain once there ran a veritable maze of trunk lines, of intermediate and secondary main lines, of branches and of mere twigs of railway. Some are now buried in urban concrete. Some have been sanitised into footpaths. Some stolen and converted into alien road, where nobody watches the trains go by, or waves to the driver . . . for there is the rub: the railway was part of the landscape – a ribbon not a scar. Railways and people went together as naturally as the horse and cart that they replaced. Now, where the railway has gone and where nature seeks again to claim her own, we may find places of solitude in which to contemplate yesteryear.

Next time you take the train, keep a watch from the window for the lingering remains of a long-gone junction. Where did that line go? Next time you drive through the countryside and cross over or under a bridge, ponder awhile. Next time you study an Ordnance Survey map, look not just for the *long barrow* or *tumuli*, but locate the 'track of old railway'.

Left
For an Uppingham School boy, afflicted with railway enthusiasm, the years 1948–52 could have been better used if his knowledge and appreciation of local railway history had been greater. Yet instead of studying the activity at Seaton we chose to walk to Manton to watch 'Jubilees' on the Midland main line.

Seaton was a secret place really. Indeed, as long ago as 1879, Seaton-Luffenham was relegated to a single-track branch: yet amazingly the $3\frac{3}{4}$ miles of rural Rutland survived to become the last steam-hauled push-and-pull service in Britain.

Yet Seaton was dominated – and still is – not by trains, but by the splendid Harringworth Viaduct straddling the Welland Valley. 1,275 yards long, the 82 arches of 40ft span are as magnificent a monument to the railway era as any structure in Britain. Here it is, on 26 October 1984.

For the villagers of Seaton and Harringworth, the sight of a train on the viaduct may sadly soon be but a memory. Seaton lost its railway about twenty years ago, and the station is now a junkyard. Midland main line trains were routed away; occasional diversions via Corby are increasingly rare. Corby itself is no longer the source of steel and iron-ore traffic. As I write these words, I am told by BR that there are no plans to close the line to freight; but one can only hope that Ribblehead today is not Harringworth tomorrow. . . .

Above right
The final section of the North Cornwall line, beside the glorious Camel estuary, opened on 27 March 1899; and closed on 30 January 1967. Amongst its most memorable features, to those of us who knew the line, was this distinctive three-span girder bridge across Little Petherick Creek about half a mile short of the terminus of 'The Withered Arm' at Padstow.

This photograph was taken in September 1980. At that time the bridge was dangerous and closed, but now it is part of the footpath on the old line. OS Sheet 200: map reference 925741.

Below right
The pillars of the abandoned nineteenth-century bridge, striding across the River Oich on the line of the erstwhile Invergarry and Fort Augustus Railway, are the most visible and most durable remains of this far-flung outpost of latter-day railway mania, by Loch Ness.

My long-nurtured desire to visit Fort Augustus coincided with a quite foul day for colour photography, in October 1983, as is self-evident. Yet for anyone for whom railway enthusiasm generates the desire to relive our nation's history, this place more than repays a visit. OS Sheet 34, map reference 376094.

Immortalised by the photographs of Ivo Peters, the Somerset and Dorset Joint Railway did and always will hold an unique place in the hearts, minds and memories of railway enthusiasts. Its demotion, downgrading, degradation, demise, dereliction and destruction is as dire and deplorable now, in retrospect, as was the disgust felt that dreadful day, 7 March 1966, when the initials S & D became part of the folk-lore of Britain's railway history. Names like Midford, Binegar, Evercreech – there is no end to the choice – live on.

To select one place to re-visit, these many years later, may seem a morbid task. In truth it is more akin to visiting a memorial than a grave, for the spirit of that line will never die. Ivo Peters has seen to that, as have innumerable other photographers including my late chum, Derek Cross. Chilcompton Tunnel, seen here, is one of those places that mean S & D: one bore is now a rifle range. No Midland Compounds or '4F's any more, but memories, memories. . . . OS Sheet 183, map reference 652523.

Locating and exploring old lines is an intensely personal business, deeply satisfying and rewarding in its ability to stir one's imagination. If one revisits places plucked from one's memory of days gone by there is an added sweetness to those pangs. He who knows not the Cleobury Mortimer and Ditton Priors Railway, knows not England. He who remembers the Uppingham branch, remembers rural Britain. There is not a county so bereft of history, of memory, that stands excluded from the search. If you have never set off to find a long-abandoned railway line, you probably have no soul, and you certainly cannot begin to appreciate our island's history.

10　Rule Britannia

Overleaf
Good fortune meteorologically often attended my shed visits in the Manchester area, and it is Patricroft shed's atmosphere rather than cloud that gives the hazy appearance, on 5 March 1965. Visible by the coaler is 'Black 5' 4–6–0 No. 44926, with 4–6–2 No. 70022 *Tornado*, a Carlisle Upperby engine at this date. This member of the class was one of those allocated to Cardiff Canton in the late 'fifties – the only former GWR depot where the 7P Pacifics were much appreciated.

Note the grab-holes in the smoke deflectors. These were inserted by Western Region to replace the handrails which were said to be reponsible for impairing the driver's visibility and causing a serious accident near Didcot.

With service on the Manchester–Glasgow expresses, Patricoft shed saw quite a few 'Britannias' in the 'sixties: by this date they were usually dirty, but had not quite reached the state of dereliction, devoid of name and even number-plates, that attended their final months.

With the wealth of detailed assessment available in numerous excellent books, it would be both inappropriate and beyond my ability to seek to add anything 'new' about the 'Britannias'. Nor indeed, is it my intention to try to assess their merits and faults in comparison with other classes. The only gap this book can claim to fill is in the use of some of my previously unpublished photographs. It should be said in their defence that the 'Britannias' entered service under the critical eye of tens of thousands of steam enthusiasts, many of whom had fanatical loyalty to 'their' railways. Then it is also true that standards of maintenance and quality of coal, let alone footplate morale, were infinitely inferior to those pertaining in the 1930s, the last period when brand new locomotive classes of similar power and style had been introduced. The exception to this was Bulleid's Pacifics, introduced in the 1940s, which themselves earned a none-too-enviable reputation initially. Indeed, those of us who eulogised the Bulleid engines, perhaps prefer to forget that, in their first year or so, they were often relegated to freight work by their shedmasters due to frequent failures. But that is another story, albeit one known to Robin Riddles.

That there is nothing new under the sun is itself an oft-repeated maxim. The appeal of the steam engine to contemporary enthusiasts seems to be heightened by the passage of time elapsed since they were the predominant form of motive power on Britain's railways. The ability to discover a new steam theme with which to capture attention is given to few. One of those few is Peter Hands who, like a human ferret in a disused mine, has hit a new seam and loosened new fuel with which to kindle the fires of interest, this time in the individual history and fate of each of the thousands of steam locomotives still in use in the last ten years of steam on British Rail. For any of those countless thousands who once collected numbers or took photographs, his series 'What Happened to Steam?' encourages us to look up our records anew:

141

in a nutshell he enables us to renew our acquaintance with, re-examine our records of, and reinvigorate our research into what we saw, by telling us more about the individual record of the object of our interest than we had perhaps realised or sought to know.

Whilst Peter Hands has toiled at the number-face, so film and camera experts have toiled at the picture-face. Perhaps my happiest moment, as I got to grips with this book, was the discovery of a rehabilitation service for some of my slides, previously catalogued with disparaging remarks about fade and discolouration. The contents of two boxes of my precious early (1963) photo-marathon had, it seemed suffered mortally, as I experimented with differing colour films. Had I been in any way knowledgeable about such matters, or known those who have subsequently advised and helped me, then certain it is that Gevacolour would never have seen the inside of my camera. Now, however, thanks to Spectrum and modern technology, once-useless material can be reinstated in my stock, and amongst the revived photographs is a number of 'Britannias', the first of the Standard Class locomotives to appear following the nationalisation of the railways. No. 70000 'Britannia' emerged from Crewe Works in January 1951, and thus began the final chapter

Number	Name	Location	Date	Home Shed at Photo-Date
70004	*William Shakespeare*	Bletchley	28.4.63	Willesden (Transferred to Carlisle Canal May 63)
70012	*John of Gaunt*	Bletchley	28.4.63	Willesden (Transferred from March that month)
70013	*Oliver Cromwell*	Carnforth Bolton	25.6.68 8.68	Carnforth Carnforth
70015	*Apollo*	Stockport	10.3.67	Stockport
70021	*Morning Star*	Willesden Wembley	3.63 6.4.63	Willesden Willesden
70022	*Tornado*	Patricroft	5.3.65	Carlisle (Upperby)
70024	*Vulcan*	Bristol	27.6.64	Crewe (North)
70026	*Polar Star*	Wembley	6.4.63	Aston
70035	*Rudyard Kipling*	Warrington	23.4.64	Carlisle (Kingmoor)
70039	*Sir Christopher Wren*	Warrington	23.4.64	Carlisle (Kingmoor)
70042	*Lord Roberts*	Bletchley	28.4.63	Willesden (Transferred to Crewe North, May 63)
70047		Watford Junction	27.4.63	Willesden
70052	*Firth of Tay*	Birkenhead	19.9.65	Banbury
70054	*Dornoch Firth*	Willesden	5.7.64	Willesden ·

of British steam locomotive design. The saga ended on Sunday 11 August 1968 when No. 70013 *Oliver Cromwell* pulled out of Manchester Victoria Station on that 15 guinea-per-head rail-tour, IT57: a journey for thriftless ghouls.

Only two 'Britannias' have featured in my previous books of steam on BR, largely as a result of the coincidental inclusion of the majority amongst the photo-casualties mentioned above. Since my photography started at the end of 1962, and as the first of the class was not withdrawn until June 1965, when No. 70007 *Coeur-de-Lion* bit the dust, it seems right that they should be given a chapter to themselves. At the foot of the previous page is a list of my 'camera sightings', a rather short list, and almost exclusively located on the London Midland Region.

Although the 'Britannias', if judged objectively, could be classified as a successful class, they faced a hurdle which, by its very nature was nearly insurmountable – namely prejudice. Whilst the act of nationalisation was political, its enactment *per se* required for its success a willingness to submerge all loyalties, to GWR, LMS, LNER and SR, not to mention the pre-grouping companies; an act that required a denial, almost a denunciation, of that attribute – company loyalty – which sets apart railways, as an industry, from any other form of industrial activity. One has only to experience the reaction of constituents to such events as joining the EEC, to imagine what 'nationalisation' meant for men like Hawksworth, Bulleid, Ivatt, Thompson; or perhaps more important, to the men for whom the Chief Mechanical Engineer (CME) was the apex of a team who wore the mantle of the generations at Swindon, Eastleigh, Crewe, or Doncaster. The first new engine to be designated 'BR' was thus unlikely to achieve uncritical acclaim.

The new British Railways policy required its Railway Executive 'to compare the differing company techniques and to standardise the best'. R. A. Riddles, board member responsible for mechanical and electrical engineering (presumably no newly-nationalised body could face the inegalitarianism implicit in the title and initials CME) wisely decided that to select from existing designs would have been, in railway terms, politically in-expedient. Like judging a beauty contest, you please one entrant and antagonise the rest! He decided therefore to opt for entirely new designs, using where appropriate the best components and practices from the Big Four companies.

That the 'Britannias' were in appearance more LMS than GWR, LNER or SR, is incontrovertible. With Riddles' own background as a Stanier man, plus his choice of R. C. Bond as Chief Officer (Locomotive Construction and Maintenance) and E. S. Cox as Executive Officer (Design) – with both of whom he had worked in

This is the first 'Gevacolour' transparency that I have dared to reproduce in any of my books. Unlike other films, this product faded and went pink and unusable, until Spectrum managed to remove some of the distortion in the colour. Please excuse the quality of this photograph, which shows the only un-named member of the class, No. 70047, at this date allocated to Aston MPD, heading north from Watford Junction on the return working of a Special to the Schoolboys' International Football Match played at Wembley Stadium on 27 April 1963.

The final batch of 'Britannias', Nos 70045–54, were turned out of Crewe Works in 1954 and were paired with the large BR1D tender which carried 9 tons of coal and were equipped with steam pushers. Note the handrails on the smoke-deflectors, to the absence of which reference is made in the previous caption.

As with all the BR Standard engines, ease of maintenance was a top priority: thus the high running-plate, which inevitably meant some sacrifice in appearance. Nevertheless, there can be little doubt that 70047, like the other 54 members of the class, looked every bit an express engine in the best British tradition, although the 'Britannia' design was probably more of an assortment, from the 'Big Four' predecessors, than any of the other BR Standard classes. Designed at Derby and built at Crewe, they were the first British two-cylinder Pacifics.

his LMS days – this was almost inevitable. Added to this must be the similarity in overall design priority, of Stanier's and Riddles' proper and understandable concern about wide route availability and design for low maintenance costs, of their respective locomotives.

As was usual, experience dictated design changes. For example, the later batches of the class to be built had larger tenders, due to operating deficiencies on some of the longer runs from sheds like Holyhead, caused by the original 7-ton tenders with inset coal bunkers. During overhaul, larger BR tenders were fitted to some of the earlier engines. Steam coal-pushers were fitted to many of the BR1D tenders, with their 9-ton coal capacity.

Numerous complaints about rough riding, dirt and draught were made by the footplatemen, and various modifications were incorporated over the years. Following a bad accident near Didcot, changes were made to the smoke deflectors on the Western Region's allocated engines, by removing the handrails in order to improve the drivers' visibility. Various sizes, shapes and placings of grab-holds were made to the deflectors, so that by the end of their reign, there was precious little 'standardisation' in this detail.

It was my immense good fortune to meet Mr Riddles; with the tenacity and brashness you would expect of a politician, I invited myself to his home in Calne. In his old age he wrote to me and, in his letter dated 21 January 1981, he replied to my request to visit him and record a conversation. Not surprisingly he was pestered and pursued by countless admirers, but although his head probably told him to reject these constant suitors, his heart was too big. He listed some of the people who were nagging him for interviews, ending his letter to me 'Tomorrow a man writing a history of Crewe is coming and I, as the last serving member of the Railway Executive, am the poor old "lemon" to be squeezed!!' Having remonstrated, he finished his handwritten note 'If you would give me a day or two's notice, I'll be available.'

I shall treasure his letter, and that interview, for ever. Indeed it would make an interesting and provocative booklet in its own right. He dealt with the politics of his early days in the newly-created BR in a way that made me feel like a spectator at the creation of a new era of railway history. Here is a brief extract from that (recorded) conversation, in which he is dealing with the point about the initial problems of designing those first Standard Class engines:

When I was given the job I hated nationalisation as much as anybody because I had a good job as Vice-President of the

LMS. I had literally no responsibility for detail at all. I just went sailing around admiring other people's work, you know. And when I took over the job on the railway at Marylebone, I was faced with four CME's, some friendly, some antagonistic, all of them absolutely frigid because they did not want any interference with their work, which is understandable, and I set up as a mediator. I thought 'what I've got to do is to get these people together somehow', so I set up a committee, or rather I discussed with the operator – what did he want; simultaneously I said I want exchange trials to see if there is a locomotive on any one region better than another, on a particular job, express or freight, and having done all that, I found out that marginally they were more or less the same. There were only two which one could consider equal and that was the 'B1' and the Black Stanier, the 'B1' of the North Eastern. Then, of course, as these things went on I realised that if I chose any one of these types as a standard I shall be in trouble with one or the other series, or a region rather. I mean there is regional loyalty.

Mr Riddles continued, and went into some detail. After further explanations he added:

Having got all that together then I said to them, to my drawing office, through design assistants, I said 'Now we've got to get down to the arrangement we want, get them to work it out.' Well, we won't know if we can. In that Britannia I put a bit of Great Western, LMS, there was a bit of North Eastern and bit of my old engine. I said that the driver has got to have a seat, which upset the Great Western drivers. Believe it or not, they had never sat down before!

By 'my old engine' Riddles was referring to his 'Austerity' 2–8–0 and 2–10–0.

Perceptive readers will have noticed no mention by Riddles, in the extract quoted, of the Southern. He had plenty to say about Bulleid, indeed he had personal reminiscences about many of the great names of the locomotive world; but this chapter is about his 'Britannia's. I asked him why, out of the 55 'Britannia's only one, No. 70047, was never named. 'I have not the faintest idea,' he said, and when I pursued the subject, he added 'I have not the remotest idea because quite frankly I never took a great deal of interest in the naming of them, because that was mainly the publicity side. Then I wasn't concerned. The first one, old Barnes did it, he named "Britannia" as you know.'

(As an aside, it is not universally known that, when 70000

Overleaf
Officially designed as mixed-traffic express locomotives, the Britannias inevitably earned their spurs, and were most photographed, on the main-line passenger trains to which they were allocated in their early years. With the rapid and insidious spread of the main-line diesels their appearances on express passenger trains in the London area in their last few years became infrequent, although they could occasionally be seen on special duties such as that seen on page 146.

With the sole exception of *Oliver Cromwell* (see page 152), the last survivors were based at Carlisle Kingmoor and were withdrawn at the end of 1967. One of these was No. 70021 *Morning Star*, seen here with steam to spare some years earlier – on 6 April 1963 to be precise – with a fitted freight at Wembley. Originally allocated to Laira (from which depot the Britannias became the largest engines ever to work in Cornwall), *Morning Star* was 'on the books' at Willesden at the date of this photograph. She was one of the Western Region engines that did not have the smoke-deflector handrails removed (see caption on page 141).

This may be one of the last photographs taken on the LNWR main line before the overhead electric paraphernalia so changed the landscape.

Britannia was named, at Marylebone on 30 January 1951 by Alfred Barnes, Minister of Transport, LMS Jubilee No. 45700, which had until then carried that name, was re-named *Amethyst* – in memory of contemporary drama on the Yangtze).

Re-reading that 'interview', of which the few sentences quoted here are but a tiny sample, makes me realise how very fortunate I was to enjoy the company of a great man for some two hours. What a witty and perceptive gentleman. He further mentioned the 'Britannias' during the course of his explanation about the relationship between driver technique and locomotive efficiency.

RAR The trouble is that, as I said, the locomotive was simple machinery and it's not a matter of size, it's a matter of art, and unless and until you've got experience of knowing how they act in service, nobody can report to you exactly what's happening, you've got to be there, and the whole point was that whereas on the testing plants they'd say this engine burns 5% more coal and is that much less efficient and so on, in practice I always used to say, a fireman has only got to put on 11 shovelfuls of coal between Euston and Birmingham to increase the consumption a pound a mile and the only difference is to have a jolly good boiler which steams well, and it proves, as a matter of fact, 'Britannias', when they were on the Western, they varied hundreds of pounds of coal, on the same journey with different engines.

RA Mind you, of course, those 'Britannias' were heartily disliked on the Western really, weren't they initially, because . . .

RAR It was only prejudice.

RA Oh, yes, I'm certain.

RAR Because when they went on the Eastern they revolutionised the lines.

It is now a matter of recorded history how well the 'Britannias' were received, and how well they performed, on the East Anglian main lines; but they took over from the 'B17's whereas on the Western they were expected to outperform the 'Castles', a very different kettle of fish from a 'B17'. So it came down in the end perhaps to prejudice based on predecessor locomotives.

By the time I saw and photographed my first 'Britannia', steam was already under sentence. No more were they immaculate, hauling crack expresses like the 'Hook Continental', 'Mancunian', 'Golden Arrow' or 'Red Dragon'. My memories are of proud locomotives humbled by neglect. For some reason, even by

the standards of filth that were sadly the hallmark of the dwindling steam stock, the Riddles' Pacifics that came my way seemed destined to be consistently grimy. In spite of that, they retained their imposing appearance. One could not ignore a Britannia, in spite of coupled wheels of only 6ft 2in diameter.

As the diesels and electrics took over, the 'Britannias' were relegated from express passenger to more humdrum and less exacting roles, although they were still handling much main line passenger work in the early '60s. There was a good chance of seeing one on such trains as Football Specials at Wembley; I recall two Saturdays in April 1963 when my good fortune was rewarded by the sight of 'Britannias' at work on the type of duties for which they were intended by Riddles.

Perhaps the most enduring memories of the class come not from the pristine locomotives of the early '50s on their glamour duties, but through the lens of Derek Cross, as, neglected and forlorn they struggled up Shap or across Batty Moss viaduct: lonely, weary, resigned to being the last representative in BR service, of the 4–6–2 wheel arrangement. The initials GWR or LMS aroused strong passions and fierce emotion: not so the prosaic 'BR'. So nobody really loved the 'Britannia's with the passionate feelings evinced for an 'A4' or a 'Coronation'. Perhaps as a product of the nationalised railway, they were somewhat impersonal. If so, it was not their fault.

Born into the era of turmoil on Britain's railways, their brief time at the top soon gave way to the rejection of steam. They never really had a fair chance, over their eligible life span, to prove their pedigree.

Left
It is fitting that the last — and rather over-exposed — of my quartet of 'Britannia' photographs features No. 70013 *Oliver Cromwell*. On 2 February 1967 this locomotive emerged from the erecting shop at Crewe Works to become the last of its steam locomotives to be overhauled by British Rail. Thus did 70013 earn a place in the history books, and was subsequently and frequently used on rail tours and special duties towards the end of steam on BR, leading up to that melancholy working 1T57 on the final fling, at 15 guineas per head, on Sunday 11 August 1968.

A few days previously, *Oliver Cromwell* approaches Bolton on yet another special. Note the splendid signal-box. By this time with name painted on smoke deflectors, 70013's appearance was attended by a mournful but dignified crowd of spectators, paying homage not just to the last Pacific, but to much more: to the end of the steam era in Britain. Never again can there be created that depth of relationship between man and one of his own inventions, which served him faithfully and well for a century and a half.

Opposite
This diminutive Hunslet 0–6–0T, photographed in September 1984, was delivered for the construction of the Cyprus Government Railway in 1904. Thereafter it became locomotive Number 1 on the railway. Withdrawn from active service in the 'thirties, it was used for raising steam at Famagusta shed or workshops, and was out of commission from 1936–39. However, the Second World

11

Corner of a Foreign Field

War saw a considerable increase in traffic, and No. 1 was put back to work after overhaul. She continued in service until the railway closed in 1951. In 1953, No. 1 was confirmed for preservation, restoration taking place in 1972 by 48 Command Workshop of the Royal Electrical and Mechanical Engineers. She is seen on her plinth in Famagusta. (See page 14.)

Traditionally my final chapter comprises photographs of Barry engines. Happily, the number of locomotives in Dai Woodham's scrapyard continues to diminish, not in the heat of the cutter's torch, but through the burning enthusiasm of determined individuals smitten with passion for steam, yet undeterred by the strictures of the rich aristocrats of the railway preservation movement. These latter, who would dictate where other people's savings should be spent, have perhaps forgotten, if ever they knew, the emotions stirred by the sight of a derelict steam locomotive. Their argument is that 'funds used to buy these rotting hulks could be put to better use on the successful preserved railways'. (What 'they' mean is that 'they' want to

dictate the use of monies raised, by other people, to satisfy their own individual ambitions: 'don't do as I do, do as I say'.) The fallacy, let alone the morality of that argument was highlighted by Harvey's rescue of *King Edward II*. That was their decision, with their money. If it had not been thus decided, that £21,000 would not have been donated to the Severn Valley Railway, for instance.

As therefore the end of steam on BR in 1968 forced our attention to overseas railways, it may yet come to pass that the clearance of Barry could broaden the search for graveyards of steam. If so, this chapter may be a trailer for such a development.

Notwithstanding the undoubted and fundamental difference between a 'real' as opposed to a 'preserved' railway, there is only a fraction of the interest in foreign railways, as compared to the native variety, amongst British enthusiasts. Books on the GWR or LMS will always dwarf into insignificance the sales of a book on Indian, Chinese or Turkish railways. But what about books on derelict British-built engines or derelict British-built railways, overseas, as compared to foreign matter? Is there an as-yet-undiscovered market, awaiting some far-sighted photographer backed by an imaginative publisher with a gambler's instinct!

This rambling soliloquy attempts merely to mask with words

I am cheating here, as of course the Southern Railway 'USA' 0–6–0T locomotives were, as their classification implies, not British at all. However, as stated on page 14), it is my intention to include in this final chapter 'engines once a familiar sight in Southampton Docks, and latterly at Guildford shed'. I saw two oil-fired 'USA' 0–6–0 tanks – part of the Greek Strategic Reserve – on shed at Thessaloniki in September 1983. There were some dumped in that city, amongst many old continental designs: remember them . . . ?

Thessaloniki again, but this time, Robin Riddles' 'Austerity' 2–10–0, my long lens and a vivid imagination may create the illusion of a British-built locomotive pulling slowly through the yard. As ever, Brian Haresnape provides both readable and factual information, and his sections on these 2–10–0's in *Ivatt and Riddles Locomotives* includes both detail and well-captioned photographs. 16 of the big 'Austerities' went to Egypt in 1944, and later these were acquired by the Greeks, becoming Hellenic State Railways L6 Class Nos 951–966. Amongst the fittings of these North British Locomotive Company-built locomotives, visible still on some of the engines in September 1983, is the deflector behind the chimney. The headlight, however, has disappeared. Haresnape's careful research enables one to identify individual engines' WD numbers, by their Greek numbers.

By 1976, these Greek 'Austerities' had finished their regular passenger duties, but some were kept in working order: the last believed to be L6 No. 964 as standby engine in Alexandropolis. They were still clearly and easily identifiable on my pilgrimage to Thessaloniki: in a corner of a foreign field. . . .

my intention to conclude this book with pictures of engines wreathed not by the salt-laden mists blown off the Bristol Channel, but by the dust-laden zephyrs of more oriental climes. Only a few can claim direct British heritage. The Hedjaz Railway however, was largely destroyed by Lawrence: whilst 'USA' 0–6–0 tanks in Greece remind one of their sisters on the Southern Railway. Am I not allowed a little imaginative licence? . . .

No words of mine are able adequately to convey the spirit of a dead engine, to an enthusiast with soul. My poetry thus intended, in *In Search of Steam*, earned few friends and the 'accolade' from Jane of the worst poetry written in England this century. Perhaps the words of Rupert Brooke are a more appropriate epitaph, not just to British locomotives, but to the steam engine itself, which even in death I praise . . .

If I should die, think only this of me:
That there's some corner of a foreign field
That is for ever England. There shall be
In that rich earth a richer dust concealed;
A dust whom England bore, shaped, made aware,
Gave, once, her flowers to love, her ways to roam.
A body of England's, breathing English air,
Washed by the rivers, burnt by suns of home.
And think this heart, all evil shed away,
A pulse in the eternal mind, no less
Given somewhere back the thoughts by England given.
Her sights and sounds; dreams happy as her day;
And laughter, learnt of friends; and gentleness,
In hearts at peace, under an English heaven.

Rupert Brooke

Index

It is *not* intended to index every place, event or locomotive mentioned in the text. The post-grouping 'Big Four' are not indexed, to avoid repetition: nor are the British rail regions, or BR itself.

Generally, people and places relevant to the photography and narrative are included. Items featured in the photographs, are referred to in bold type.